RECONSTRUCTING PRACTI

This book argues that the discipline of practical theology needs to be re-shaped in the light of the impact of various influences created through the encounter with globalization. Essential to this is an engagement with the insights of other disciplines, e.g. sociology, politics, economics and philosophy. The content and authority of the Christian tradition is being challenged by the blurred encounters with more fluid lifestyles, alternative spiritualities and indeed other faiths as mediated through information technology and the breakdown of attachments to all forms of institutional life. Traditional ways of 'belonging' and relating to places and structures are being eroded leaving the established patterns of ministry, worship and church organization the province of an ageing population, while those who are now more inclined to search for 'communities of interest' avoid being drawn into the practices and structures of formal religion. What is the future for practical theology in this rapidly changing context? By examining the familiar concerns of the subject John Reader shows how it is in danger of operating with 'zombie categories' – still alive but only just – and presents the possibilities for a reflexive spirituality grounded in the Christian tradition as a way into the future.

Explorations in Practical, Pastoral and Empirical Theology

Series Editors: Leslie J. Francis, University of Warwick, UK
and Jeff Astley, Director of the North of England
Institute for Christian Education, UK

Theological reflection on the church's practice is now recognised as a significant element in theological studies in the academy and seminary. Ashgate's new series in practical, pastoral and empirical theology seeks to foster this resurgence of interest and encourage new developments in practical and applied aspects of theology worldwide. This timely series draws together a wide range of disciplinary approaches and empirical studies to embrace contemporary developments including: the expansion of research in empirical theology, psychological theology, ministry studies, public theology, Christian education and faith development; key issues of contemporary society such as health, ethics and the environment; and more traditional areas of concern such as pastoral care and counselling.

Other titles in the series include:

Deaf Liberation Theology
Hannah Lewis
978-0-7546-5524-4

Theological Reflection and Education for Ministry
The Search for Integration in Theology
John E. Paver
978-0-7546-5754-5

Renewing Pastoral Practice
Trinitarian Perspectives on Pastoral Care and Counselling
Neil Pembroke
978-0-7546-5565-7

Engaging with Contemporary Culture
Christianity, Theology and the Concrete Church
Martyn Percy
978-0-7546-3259-7

Evangelicals Etcetera
Conflict and Conviction in the Church of England's Parties
Kelvin Randall
978-0-7546-5215-1

Reconstructing Practical Theology
The Impact of Globalization

JOHN READER
Anglican Priest and Rural Officer for the Diocese of Chester, UK,
Associate Researcher with the William Temple Foundation

ASHGATE

Published by
Ashgate Publishing Limited
Gower House
Croft Road
Aldershot
Hampshire GU11 3HR
England

Ashgate Publishing Company
Suite 420
101 Cherry Street
Burlington, VT 05401-4405
USA

Ashgate website: http://www.ashgate.com

British Library Cataloguing in Publication Data
Reader, John
Reconstructing practical theology : the impact of globalization. – (Explorations in practical, pastoral and empirical theology) 1. Theology, Practical 2. Pastoral theology 3. Globalization – Religious aspects – Christianity
I. Title
253

Library of Congress Cataloging-in-Publication Data
Reader, John.
Reconstructing practical theology : the impact of globalization / John Reader.
p. cm. – (Explorations in practical, pastoral, and empirical theology.)
Includes bibliographical references and index.
ISBN 978-0-7546-6224-2 (hardcover : alk. paper)– ISBN 978-0-7546-6660-8 (paper cover : alk. paper)
1. Theology, Practical. 2. Pastoral theology. 3. Globalization–Religious aspects–Christianity. I. Title.

BV3.R325 2008
253—dc22

2007052595

ISBN 978 0 7546 6660 8 (Pbk)
ISBN 978 0 7546 6224 2 (Hbk)

Printed and bound in Great Britain by MPG Books Ltd. Bodmin, Cornwall.

Contents

Chapter 1

A Changing World

Introduction

The objective of this book is to review and refine practical theology in the light of the contemporary context in which Christianity is operating. I will argue that one of the reasons why our responses are becoming inadequate is that we are using inappropriate and dated categories to understand and describe that context, and I will then offer alternatives to those drawing on other disciplines. Broadly speaking the best way of grasping these changes is under the heading of a family of concepts derived from the study of globalization. This is another of those terms that has now swept into academic discourse and suffers from over-exposure and under-theorization, so that will also be addressed at points in the argument.

A leading contemporary sociologist, Ulrich Beck, has coined the phrase 'zombie categories' as a way of pointing to the continued employment of concepts that no longer do justice to the world we experience and yet which are difficult to abandon because of tradition and also because they are not yet totally redundant (Beck and Beck-Gernsheim 2002: 203–206). Zombie categories are 'the living dead', the tried and familiar frameworks of interpretation that have served us well for many years and continue to haunt our thoughts and analyses, even though they are embedded in a world that is passing away before our eyes. Finding convincing replacements for them however is not easy as it requires changes of discourse and changes of perception. We are likely to resist such changes and rapidly resort to the tried, tested and familiar when the challenge becomes too uncomfortable. The areas to be addressed will be outlined shortly.

Can the wider claim that globalization and its related concepts have so changed the world in which we operate really be justified? Once again this question will receive more substantial attention throughout the book.

Leaving aside for a moment a direct study of the role of Christianity and religions more generally within this changing configuration, here is a brief description from a recent text which claims to identify the hidden agenda beneath globalization. Dennis Smith argues that unless globalization changes direction within the near future the consequences will be a loss of freedoms and a damaging impact upon the struggle for human rights. In fact, 'if we go on as we are, there is a high risk of a major world war occurring by mid-century. It all depends upon who wins the current political struggle' (Smith 2006: 1).

This is not a book which indulges in sensationalist scaremongering or which foretells the end of civilization as we know it, but rather it engages in close and thoughtful historical and political analysis of current movements in globalization based on wider historical perspectives. Smith's argument is that the crucial battle is not between the West and various terrorist activists, but within the West itself. On one side are the supporters of what he calls decent democracy, a system delivering dignity, freedom and fair treatment to all citizens and, on the other, the proponents of a liberated capitalism, pursuing narrowly economic objectives but enforced by certain state and commercial interests. The 'logic of the market' currently identified with the Washington consensus and the direction being forged by the USA internationally, will be ranged against the supporters of a humane form of cosmopolitanism based upon a human rights regime and wishing to extend the benefits of growth to all, not just the fortunate few.

Using the themes of humiliation, rejection and victimization, Smith presents the case that we are heading into an unstable political environment where the hegemony of the USA will increasingly come under challenge from other major economic and political power blocs. Hence the EU, the growing power of China and India, let alone a resurgent Russia and possibly even Brazil, will soon be vying for more dominant roles within the global economy. How will the USA respond to these challenges? Smith offers a disturbing scenario:

> If urban citizens throughout the world are denied decent democracy, if they are humiliated by the logic of the global market, then they will be tempted to follow new Hitlers, promising the rewards of revenge. It has happened before. If it happens again, we will be on our way to a third world war involving the American state, terrified of humiliating decline, and its increasingly powerful global neighbours in Europe and Asia. (Smith 2006: 2)

Hopefully this is a worst-case scenario, although one can readily see how Smith reads this prediction out of the current situation. There are of course other global problems which he does not mention, notably fears of environmental disasters of various sorts and the possible struggle to command the scarce natural resources of oil, gas and water which may yet 'fuel' such global conflicts.

What has any of this got to do with religion, let alone practical theology? Religion is a powerful catalyst and source of ideas and motivation within these potential global conflicts. The USA and the George W. Bush administration is a case in point. The EU appears to be taking a much more secularist stance, but that in itself is creating tensions for both Christians and Muslims within its borders. Clearly the role of radical forms of Islam, let alone their influence in some of the most populous nations in the world, has to be taken into account within global politics. Whether it is for good or for evil – and it is probably both – religion is not going to stay off the global stage. I suggest that a practical theology that cannot grasp this dimension of its significance in world events is seriously deficient.

A Sustainable World?

Another major challenge that practical theology cannot afford to ignore comes from concerns about our relationship to the planet which we inhabit and, therefore, questions about the future of our species. The term 'sustainability' probably sums up this area of concern better than any other. We need to ponder whether or not sustainability is in any sense a Christian or theological concept, but, at the moment, it is so deeply embedded in the secular discourses with which we must engage that it is impossible to neglect it. Is our current way of life sustainable? If it is not, then any religious response is bound to be drawn into the consequences of such a conclusion. What will happen if we carry on as we are and, if the answer is that we are heading for environmental disaster, do we have the political will let alone the technical capacity to avert this?

If, again, this would appear to be a case of sensationalist scaremongering and of the more extreme suggestion that a politics of fear is being deliberately employed by Western governments, who are afraid of losing their grip over an apathetic or disillusioned populace, then one can do worse than attend to the findings of the Stern Report which was published in the autumn of 2006.

This report was commissioned by the UK government in order to present the economic case for environmental reform. Whether or not one agrees with it or is sympathetic to its general approach, the important thing is that such a report exists at all and that it will become an established part of the political and economic discourse of which we must take note.

The opening paragraphs of the executive summary provide a stark warning about what might lie ahead:

> The scientific evidence is now overwhelming: climate change is a serious global threat, and it demands an urgent global response. This review has assessed a wide range of evidence on the impacts of climate change and on the economic costs, and has used a number of different techniques to assess costs and risks. From all of these perspectives, the evidence gathered by the Review leads to a simple conclusion: the benefits of strong and early action far outweigh the economic costs of not acting. (Stern 2006: vi)

Strong and decisive action needs to be taken now if the worst effects of this are to be avoided and access to the basic elements of life for people around the world, such as water, food production, health and the environment itself is to be guaranteed. The Stern Report estimated that hundreds of millions of people will suffer if global warming is allowed to increase unchecked. This, it is claimed, can now be measured in economic terms; the failure to act will be equivalent to losing at least 5 per cent of global GDP for each successive year. One can inflate this figure to 20 per cent by including a wider range of risks and impacts. However, the costs of acting now, which would mean reducing greenhouse emissions to avoid the worst impacts of climate change, can be limited to around 1 per cent of global GDP per year.

Now one can clearly argue about such figures and the bases for their calculation, and one could criticize the very exercise of reducing environmental issues to economics, but that is not the point for our purposes. A document of this nature would have been unthinkable a few years ago. The argument is that the world has changed and that there is a growing perception and belief that humanity faces a level of risk previously unheard of, so much so that even politically motivated economists are taking this seriously and that decisions will be made on the basis of reports such as this. It is as if there is shadow hanging over us and, even though we may choose to ignore it as we go about our daily lives, it is still there and beginning to dominate our thoughts and feelings about our current and future world. It is part of our subconscious and increasingly part of our conscious lives. It is an element of a changing context which any practical theology must acknowledge and to which it must give proper attention.

The other thing that must be emphasized is that this problem is global and demands a global response. Hence the report states:

> Because climate change is a global problem, the response to it must be international. It must be based on a shared vision of long-term goals and agreement on frameworks that will accelerate action over the next decade, and it must build upon mutually reinforcing approaches at national, regional and international level. (Stern 2006: vi)

This reinforces Beck's argument about zombie categories. To begin to see the world in a new way is essential to an adequate response to this type of global risk. Environmental dangers do not obey national border controls. The nation state is no longer the most effective political unit to tackle this threat. But nation states are what we still have, alongside a growing body of international organizations, both governmental and non-governmental. Mobilizing and organizing the latter in ways that still retain a democratic ethos is a major challenge. One can see that shifting from the zombie categories to new structures for thinking and acting is not going to be easy. What are practical theology's zombie categories and how are we working to replace them with more appropriate ones? For the time being it is as if we have to learn to live in parallel worlds, the old, familiar and increasingly redundant living uncomfortably alongside the new, emerging and untested. This is not an easy place to be.

The Contours of Practical Theology

Before it is argued that practical theology is now beset by zombie categories that leave us in this strange interim location, we need to look more closely at the discipline as it is now and how it has developed in recent years. It would not overstate the case to say that this is a contested area where one encounters a wide variety of interpretations and views. What exactly falls within the remit of this subject and is there anything that might not count as practical theology?

One clear point of overlap is with what is known as pastoral theology and, without going into the details of this debate, it does need to be registered that attempts to draw a sharp distinction between the two appear somewhat fruitless. A recent standard textbook on the two subjects *The Blackwell Reader in Pastoral and Practical Theology* does not even try to separate them in its title but acknowledges the almost symbiotic relationship between the two (Woodward and Pattison 2000).

When it comes to defining practical theology the task becomes even more complex:

> In principle, the scope of practical theology is almost infinite. Any issue that is of practical contemporary human and religious concern may become the focus for practical theological consideration. Often, the kinds of issues that most concern practical theologians are those that relate to or become problematic in the life of the church and the church's ministry. (Woodward and Pattison 2000: 8)

It might seem then that one has a free hand in discussing just about anything that concerns church life. However, although this is a reasonable assessment of where things are now, it does need to be recognized that the discipline has had a sharper focus for most of its history. Here, for instance, is a description offered by one of the current established scholars in the field, Elaine Graham:

> Within the single discipline of practical theology were grouped the following sub-disciplines: homiletics (preaching); poimenics (pastoral care or the cure of souls); liturgics (public worship); jurisprudence (church government and discipline); and catechetics (education, usually of children). In principle it was understood that these various activities were indicative not just of the clerical or priestly office, but characteristic of the life and work of the whole church. (Graham 1996: 58)

If this gives a somewhat more confined area of study and appears to suggest that it is really about the application of theological insights and principles to the practice of church life and ministry, then this would be useful but unfortunately still misleading. The whole idea of an applied theology in which the real theologians do the hard thinking about the Christian tradition behind the scenes and then somehow pass it on to the front-line practitioners to work out what they are then supposed to do about it, simply reproduces that gap between theory and practice that has haunted practical theology from the beginning. Hence what one is now more likely to encounter are attempts to carve out and establish a distinctive territory for practical theology which has its own theoretical identity and integrity. So here is another example from one of the best known US scholars in the field who is concerned to ground practical theology in the sub-discipline of theological ethics.

> I believe that it is impossible to be practical in the sense of 'applied' without sooner or later making clear the norms that guide one's practice. In short, it is very difficult to draw a clear line between the moral and practical. So, for the purposes of this book, when I use the phrase 'practical theology', I am including Christian ethics or moral theology with a genuine concern not only to articulate norms but also to transform lives and institutions, to get down to specifics – to get practical. (Browning 2006: 57)

I am not about to dispute any of these statements, and it is important to show that the arguments I will present do stand broadly within a continuing discussion about the nature and scope of practical theology. I hope it is now clear that this is very much an open discussion being conducted at the highest level within the discipline and that there is room for legitimate debate and disagreement as to what exactly does fall within its remit. I will also show that it is a developing discipline, both in terms of its use of non-theological resources and in terms of its contact with regular church life and ministry.

Developments in Practical Theology

Part of the exercise of establishing practical theology as a discipline with its own identity is to point out that it has a lengthy and worthy heritage that can be traced back to the beginnings of the Christian church. This also helps people to realize that the discipline has changed over time and will continue to do so. For a glimpse into this dimension of the subject I turn to a text on theological reflection (Graham, Walton and Ward 2005). Introducing the term 'theological reflection' into the discussion is important as it represents what has become a main focus for debate within practical theology.

Graham, Walton and Ward suggest that the development of practical theology can usefully be divided into six broad historical periods (2005: 2–3). The earliest of these which covers the first two centuries of Christianity is based upon caring for one another within the Christian community and is concerned to build up the body of Christ. In the second phase an institutionalization of apostolic ministries is evident relating pastoral care to sacramental ministry. This coincided with the emergence of moral theology, a tradition that is still to be found within much Roman Catholic pastoral theology today.

It was the influence of the Enlightenment and the subsequent work of the Protestant theologian Schleiermacher which moved the subject onto another plane and its third stage of development. The idea of an applied theology began to take hold and the term practical theology appeared within the German academies during the eighteenth century. The fourth stage saw a rise in both professionalism and secularism at the start of the twentieth century, once again related to the role of the minister as a pastoral professional carrying out the tasks of ministry on behalf of the Christian community.

This brings the account almost up to date. Over the last 50 years the introduction of ideas from the fields of psychology and other sources of therapeutic knowledge has been a major influence upon practical and pastoral theology. In other words, the study of the human person has understandably figured within the development of the subject. But even this has now partly been overtaken by what Graham, Walton and Ward term the hermeneutic model of pastoral engagement, hence the increased importance of theological reflection within the discipline. This represents a move away from the clerically dominated view of pastoral care and the consequent emphasis upon other ways in which the wider church engages with its social and political context. This helps us to understand that the scope of practical theology has been broadening over the last 100 years and that one of the critical questions is that of how it relates to, draws upon and possibly critiques the insights of non-theological disciplines that touch upon its traditional areas of concern. However, the main focus of practical theology is still that of pastoral ministry, whether exercised by clergy or laity, and ways in which this contributes to the vision of the kingdom of God in the world. The implied question is whether these are now becoming zombie categories that are running alongside much broader concerns that are starting to impinge upon Christian witness and ministry.

Before moving on to examine some recent definitions of the subject area it is worth noting Graham, Walton and Ward's further description of the current types of theological reflection (2005: 12–13). These form the substance of their text and are valuable as a drawing together of a wide variety of theological approaches. The chapters cover: theology by heart – the use of personal experience, journaling and other such 'living human documents'; speaking in parables and the use of Scripture generally to offer resources for Christian reflection; telling God's story in which those

Scriptures take on an obviously normative and authoritative role through the power of narrative to define identity and belonging; writing the body of Christ and the use of corporate liturgy and the life of the gathered congregation as the primary source of theological reflection. The final three are: speaking of God in public and engaging with other disciplines as ways into interpreting the demands of Christian ministry today; theology in action or praxis as developed from the insights of liberation theology and the work of people like Freire and finally the construction of local or vernacular theologies which take the particular local context as the touchstone of theological reflection (Reader 1994). Again, what emerges clearly from this is the issue of how much practical theology is going to engage with the ideas of other disciplines and then either reject them or incorporate them into its own processes of reflection. We are not simply talking about the psychological and therapeutic but also the sociological, the economic and the political. This is where practical theology has got to now.

The Characteristics of Practical Theology

To complete the picture of current thinking about practical theology I return to the reader in pastoral and practical theology referred to earlier (Woodward and Pattison 2000).The two editors emphasize again that the field is a diverse and contested one in which a variety of approaches can be identified. However, they still want to draw out a number of central characteristics that will aid in interpreting this subject area, (Woodward and Pattison 2000: 13–16). I will mention only some of these in order to illustrate the general direction of their argument.

First, practical theology is transformational in that it aims to make a difference not just to people, but also to understandings and situations in the contemporary world. In order to do this effectively it has to look beyond the purely rational and logical to take into account the affective aspects of human behaviour and the more creative ways in which insights about pastoral situations can be expressed. However, it does this from a particular perspective, that of the Christian tradition from which it has emerged. Yet this also involves an honesty about the limits of its knowledge and understanding. Difficult questions about human suffering and justice cannot be given slick and easy answers, but the depth of experience which lies behind them has to be taken into account.

In terms of method, practical theology is unsystematic because it is engaging with a fragmented and complex world which is in a state of constant flux. The authors describe this as a 'throwaway theology' which must be flexible and provisional as its context both in terms of church and world continues to change. It follows from this that it is also responsive to context and to the development of forms of local theology, even though it refers back to the documents and practices of the Christian tradition. Practical theology is socio-politically aware and committed to engaging with real problems, often from a grass-roots perspective. This is where theological reflection comes into play as Christians are encouraged to analyse, respond to and develop critiques of current practice which are perceived to be damaging to human life.

Finally, it is interdisciplinary.

> It uses the methods and insights of academic and other disciplines that are not overtly theological as part of its theological method. Theology, in itself, it is maintained, cannot reveal all that one needs to know adequately to respond to contemporary situations and issues. Thus economics, sociology, psychology, and other disciplinary findings and perspectives must be utilized. (Woodward and Pattison 2000: 15)

This makes practical theology a demanding subject to study and practise according to these authors, and raises questions about how such non-theological insights are to be related to the more strictly theological. One can see from this that a very particular interpretation and approach to this area is being advocated here, much closer to the last three developments as outlined by Graham, Walton and Ward. I would certainly place myself within this broad approach and agree that practical theology must draw upon other disciplines if it is to come to grips with the context in which it now operates. What I will argue in due course is that the family of concepts encountered through the study of globalization now demands from practical theology a further level of analysis and debate with which it has yet to fully engage. But this is going to be a reconstruction that builds upon much that has gone before even though it will question some of the categories familiar to students of practical theology.

If one still believes that a definition is of some value then I will recall the way in which I tried to describe my understanding of a local, rural theology, back in the 1980s. I reached the conclusion that it could be presented as 'critical, emancipatory, Christian, practice' (Reader 1986: 52). This contained all the essential elements of the task, the practical engagement, the grounding within the Christian tradition, and then the questioning edge to interpretation leading to an understanding based upon the freedom promised by the kingdom of God, or what I would now call 'the messianic'. I note that a recent text on practical theology suggests a not dissimilar definition:

> Practical theology is critical, theological reflection on the practices of the Church as they interact with the practices of the world, with a view to ensuring and enabling faithful participation in God's redemptive practices in, to and for the world. (Swinton and Mowat 2006: 6)

That seems a sound base from which to launch out into the deeps of globalization to see where this journey of theological reflection might take us.

Emerging Themes for Practical Theology

We begin by identifying the areas in which globalization is having an impact upon practical theology and to lay out the territory which will be explored in the rest of the book. It needs to be re-emphasized that even though the existing categories of parish and pastoral work, worship, preaching and teaching and concern for young people appear to be losing their hold and turning into zombie categories, they are still of importance and will feature in practical theology for some time to come. The themes that I am about to describe are not, as yet, straightforward replacements for the familiar areas of study, but run alongside them and raise questions about their future value. These emerging themes are essentially interlocking and attempts to draw strict demarcation lines between them will seem somewhat artificial. I will highlight three in this introductory chapter and elaborate upon them at later stages in the book.

The first is that of the blurring of boundaries characteristic of recent reflections upon globalization and which is beginning to become visible within practical theology also. The second is that of the tension between enclosures and thresholds and which relates directly to the emancipatory and transformatory dimensions of practical theology. The third is what is called reflexivity and its relationship to the tasks and self-understanding of theological reflection. Running through each of these are the twin themes of sustainability from the secular world and hospitality from the world of faith. Most of what follows will be pursuing these interlocking themes in the changing context of globalization.

Blurred Boundaries

Both sociological and political studies of globalization frequently refer to the fact that the traditional boundaries of nation states and other political organizations are being crossed regularly by a whole series of issues. It has already been pointed out that environmental problems for instance are no respecters of national borders, but the same is also true for the flows of global finance and business, let alone the threat constituted by international terrorism. However, there is a further level of discussion that will impinge upon our particular study and that involves more methodological consideration. Are the boundaries and distinctions that are normally drawn within the academic study of sociology and politics any longer adequate to capture the complexity of what is now happening?

Returning to the work of Ulrich Beck, we can draw out the significance of this question. He challenges the very structure of either/or thinking that has been central to a series of academic studies, not just sociology but also socio-biology and ethnology (Beck 2006: 5). The classic argument has been that drawing sharp divisions between different groups, tribes, religions, classes or families is essential to understanding the preconditions for identity, politics, society, community and even democracy. 'It assumes that a space defended by (mental) fences is an indispensable precondition for the formation of self-consciousness and for social integration' (Beck 2006: 5). In other words, we can only know who we are if it is possible to draw clear boundaries between 'us and them'; we construct our individual and collective identities by knowing who is different from us and putting them in another category.

Beck argues that this theory is empirically false and arose from the political conditions of a particular stage of development, that of the clearly demarcated nation state. But this division no longer holds because it is now clear that our response to the suffering of others can no longer be limited by these criteria. He talks about the existence of a cosmopolitan empathy such as that which fuelled the protest across the globe against the war in Iraq in 2003 and the general perception that conflicts in one part of the world have a direct impact upon what happens elsewhere and are often the result of decisions made in distant corridors of power. This means that more of us are able to place ourselves in the position of distant others whose lives have previously seemed very remote from our own. The presence of the media in these places and the appearance of often live pictures during the course of these events is another contributory factor.

However, as Beck argues, this does not mean the demise of national boundaries and sympathies. On the contrary, cosmopolitan and national empathy 'permeate, enhance, transform and colour each other' (Beck 2006: 6). What is taking place is a blurring of the boundaries where the new and the old coexist within a new and shifting configuration. This requires of sociologists a revision of the traditional framework of nation state and the other divisions which have been central to its study of human societies. This includes such themes as the 'civilizational community of fate' which acknowledges that threats cross national boundaries; the impossibility of living in a world society without borders and the resulting compulsion to redraw old boundaries and rebuild old walls as a defence against change; and what he calls the melange principle:

> The principle that local, national, ethnic, religious and cosmopolitan cultures and traditions interpenetrate, interconnect and intermingle – cosmopolitanism without provincialism is empty, provincialism without cosmopolitanism is blind. (Beck 2006: 7)

The more the boundaries become porous and blurred, the more people will feel the need to establish differences clearly and distinctly and yet the attempts to do so will meet with resistance. Thus the academic study of society and politics requires conceptual tools that can acknowledge this internal conflict and the contradictions that arise from it. The so-called 'war on terror' is a good case in point. It is being fought and presented by governments as if it was still a conventional war that can be fought by traditional national forces against a similar enemy, but everybody knows that it is not like that any longer, yet the new configurations taking shape cannot be fitted into existing categories of interpretation.

> Along with the threats goes the inability of existing institutions to respond to them. Thus, as the danger grows, it becomes harder to resist the temptation to deny the danger or to normalize it into a form that fits the established categories for its prevention. (Beck 2006: 40)

The only way in which the existing nation states can digest and begin to cope with this new threat is by placing it within existing and comfortable categories and by pursuing the conflict within those familiar terms. So terrorism is identified with so-called 'rogue states' that are then put under pressure through sanctions and the further threat of military action. The battle is presented as state against state, even though it is no longer of this nature. Only in this way can the USA for instance still feel secure in the face of a new and disturbing danger.

This blurring of boundaries is also recognizable however from within the field of culture. Beck refers to a piece of research that has shown that:

> More and more people are quite conscious of the fact that they are living in an age of global flows of money and goods and boundless risks; that interdependencies with other human

> beings, places and environments are on the increase, that the boundaries of nations, cultures and religions are blurring and intermingling; and that they are inextricably intertwined in an experiential space in which local, national and global influences interpenetrate. (Beck 2006: 43)

Rather than a 'monogamy of space' characteristic of the earlier modern age we now have a 'polygamy of space' in which people's contacts and loyalties are multiple and shifting rather than single and static. E-mail is perhaps the most powerful symbol of this: not simply the capacity to contact family and friends across the globe but also the opportunity to establish links with unknown and distant others and then to pursue those relationships without any face-to-face contact. As is well documented this brings with it new risks as well as exciting possibilities.

How does any of this affect practical theology and its traditional concerns? This will be pursued in later chapters but I now give two examples. A family one of whose sons and his wife and children have had to emigrate to Australia because the company he worked for insisted they relocate, tell me that they are still in regular contact through Skype and able to talk to each other more effectively than by phone call within the country. In addition, because the head office is still in Europe, regular trips back can be combined with a quick flight across to the UK and a drive up the motorway. So what would have been a real bereavement and sense of loss with part of the family living on the opposite side of the world is suddenly nothing like such a wrench despite distance and potential loss of contact. Pastoral care takes on different dimensions in this new world of blurred boundaries.

A further example is that of the traditional division within church life and ministry between urban and rural. One only has to read recent reports on church life such as *Faithful Cities* (Commission on Urban Life and Faith 2006) to see that this division is becoming increasingly difficult to maintain. Back in 1985 with the publication of *Faith in the City* (Archbishop of Canterbury's Commission on Urban Priority Areas 1985) it appeared relatively easy to identify urban priority areas and to talk about 'the inner city' and its distinctive problems. Since then it has become obvious that smaller towns and not exclusively the major conurbations contain areas of significant deprivation. It has also been recognized that remote rural areas suffer from lack of facilities and a shortage of affordable housing and that people can be just as trapped and left behind there as in London or Manchester. Similar problems are found across the urban–rural divide although they may manifest themselves differently because of issues of scale. In the middle are various versions of 'rural suburbia' or 'ex-urban' city shadow areas where very often the most affluent and most powerful people congregate because of house prices and access to transport. These may like to present themselves as rural but what that means in practice is very different from the interpretation of rural ministry that is invariably still adhered to by church reports and training courses.

I would argue that the important boundary now is that between local and global rather than rural and urban and that even that is becoming increasingly blurred. Decisions made in other parts of the world and by distant and unknown others can have a significant impact upon who lives and works in many areas. Agriculture is a clear example of this along with what remains of much traditional manufacturing industry within the UK. If one wants to understand what is happening in people's lives within one's parish as a parish priest now, one must have some sort of a grasp of the global factors that determine and shape their working and domestic lives. More of this will emerge in due course, but I hope it is clear why this blurring of boundaries will figure throughout the book.

Enclosures and Thresholds

We have established that one of the characteristics of a contemporary practical theology is that of being an emancipatory or transformatory discipline, one that advances the freedoms associated with the kingdom of God. The question though is what this means in practical terms in the current context. What exactly is entailed by such a freedom? What is one trying to gain freedom from? In what ways are people now trapped or constrained by life as they experience it? I will use the terms 'enclosure' and 'threshold' to refer to those aspects of contemporary life that do indeed appear to hold people captive or else which offer the hope of pathways to other possibilities.

However, one needs to explain the origin of these terms and how they fit into the globalization debate, and this requires a brief foray into the world of radical politics and particularly the work of two authors, Hardt and Negri, and their analysis of current political life (Hardt and Negri 2001, 2005; Negri 2004). Their thesis is that the form in which globalization has developed has created a situation in which a capitalist economic regime has captured all aspects of our lives. In what they describe as 'Empire', they suggest that this particular regime is now all-encompassing and all-embracing, that there is no longer any 'outside' from which one can view the present or work for alternatives. We are all inside the current system, whether we recognize it or not, and that therefore if any alternatives are to develop they must be from inside the existing structures. So globalization is an enclosure and it is not easy to see how anybody can break free from this.

Central to their thesis is an examination of sovereignty and how that has changed over time (Hardt and Negri 2001: 186–9). They argue that in the passage from imperialism to Empire there is progressively less distinction between inside and outside. So in terms of territory it is no longer obvious where in the world one might have to be in order to feel outside the global capitalist system. Even civil society, the realm of family, voluntary groups, churches and other faith groups is now increasingly drawn into this world. The so-called natural order which we now think of as the environment is equally subject to commercial and economic considerations. Ideas of an inner self somehow distinct from these external forces are difficult to maintain.

This may sound deeply depressing but, in their later work (Hardt and Negri 2005), they do suggest possible ways forward through the resistance and protest of individuals and single issue groups engaged with a range of different issues.

As other political writers have commented (Habermas 1981), the distinction made by liberal politics between the public world and private spaces has been eroded:

> Public space has been privatized to such an extent that it no longer makes sense to understand social organization in terms of a dialectic between private and public spaces, between inside and outside. The place of modern liberal politics has disappeared, and thus from this perspective our postmodern and imperial society is characterized by a deficit of the political. (Hardt and Negri 2001: 188)

Even the sphere of the military and normal conflict has been enveloped within Empire. Instead of the stand-off between two global superpowers that characterized the Cold War, there is now the USA and no single, identifiable, major opponent, rather a series of elusive enemies and a constant series of crises more or less related to American economic and political dominance. This is not to say that the USA is now the Empire itself and that its power is all-embracing. Rather:

> The capitalist market is one machine that has always run counter to any division between outside and inside. It is thwarted by barriers and exclusions; it thrives instead by including always more within its sphere. Profit can be generated only through contact, engagement, interchange and commerce. The realization of the world market would constitute the point of arrival of this tendency. In its ideal form there is no outside to the world market: the entire globe is its domain. (Hardt and Negri 2001: 190)

So there is a uniform and smooth space of Empire. There is really nowhere that is not part of this system. Through the processes of modern technological transformation, even nature has become capital – note our comments about the Stern Report and its conversion of environmental problems into economic terms. Unless issues can be presented as 'bottom-line', financially driven concerns it is increasingly difficult to get them registered in public and political discourse. Faith groups are appropriated into the agenda of social capital and brought into discussions only if it can be argued that they add value to the normal processes of capitalist existence.

Two other terms used by Hardt and Negri further emphasize the stranglehold that global capitalism exercises over all aspects of life. 'Bio-power', first made familiar by Foucault, suggests that even the physical and bodily nature of our lives is now part of this all-encompassing regime. We become 'docile subjects' living our lives and imagining that we have freedom when in truth the options available to us are dictated by the needs of the market and we are slaves to a system which requires us to keep purchasing and desiring well beyond the point at which it is of real benefit to us. Even when it comes to matters of religion and spirituality, as will be seen in a later chapter, we are close to becoming consumers who crave entertainment and will abandon one tradition as soon as it no longer pleases nor satisfies. Freedom has become equated with consumer choice.

Hardt and Negri also employ the term 'full spectrum dominance' from the military world to describe the way in which the capitalist system exercises total power through its influence over culture and other aspects of civil life. But this is where Empire begins to run up against its limits:

> A sovereign power is always two-sided: a dominating power always relies on the consent or submission of the dominated. The power of sovereignty is thus always limited, and this limit can always potentially be transformed into resistance, a point of vulnerability, a threat. (Hardt and Negri 2005: 54)

Hence we return to the arguments presented by Smith about the effects of humiliation and the opposition that is engendered by all attempts at such total dominance. As Hardt and Negri say, it turns counter-insurgency into a full-time and almost impossible task as the reactions against US power continue to spring up in different places and with differing motivations. In the end full spectrum dominance creates its own seeds of destruction, and unless real political alternatives are found the prospects for any lasting global peace are remote.

Where does this connect with practical theology? If Hardt and Negri are correct then one ought to be able to see the impact of this type of power in the lives of ordinary people wherever they happen to be within Empire. I would argue that it is certainly evident in the working lives of many I encounter and the sense they often express of being trapped within a system that makes increasing demands upon them at the cost often of their family lives, let alone their capacity to engage in any voluntary activity such as church-going or support. Even the lives of the relatively affluent are determined by the requirements of the market: there are mortgages to be paid and children to be sent to the best schools so that they have a competitive edge in a hostile employment market determined by global economics. Then there are those who are the obvious victims of the system, without the stability of work or family life and perhaps living on the margins of society. Can any of us honestly say that we are outside the capitalist processes now? Hence the obvious enclosures created by current global priorities. Practical theology faces the challenge of identifying thresholds or points of engagement where alternatives become visible and faith communities may be able to nourish people in their search for the hope of transformation.

Theological Reflection and Reflexivity

Practical theology places a considerable emphasis upon the concept of theological reflection as we have already noted. However, this debate has been taken further with the references to the notion of reflexivity, which is one upon which I shall draw later in the book. Although the two ideas are related and the terms are sometimes used interchangeably, there are significant differences between them. It is important to be clear about this from the outset, so I will now present a brief examination of this subject.

If one returns to the book by Graham, Walton and Ward and their chapter on 'Theology by Heart' with particular reference to living human documents (2005: 18–46), one finds a revealing exposition of both terms. The chapter begins by arguing that theological reflection came to full realization as it encountered the development of psychology and the work of such people as Freud and William James. In other words it builds upon a practice of inner reflection and an awareness of the affective dimension of human nature and the capacity to stand back and both record and then analyse what is happening at that level. The authors then go on to say that: 'With its stress on the importance of the self as it finds expression through texts, the notion of reflexivity becomes a key word in this method of theological reflection' (Graham, Walton and Ward 2005: 19).

They go on to point out that there is a danger of encouraging an overly individualistic approach to theological reflection and that it needs to be acknowledged that this practice of inner reflection takes place within the context of the Christian community and in the light of the insights of the Christian tradition. Psalm 139 is quoted as an example of how a text can be employed in this way, where the self is placed in the setting of God's purposes and yet where it is also attributed dignity and worth in its own right. They conclude that:

> This inward movement illustrates what we will later explore as reflexivity: the concern to understand more deeply the ways of the self, positioned within the networks of society. Here, created by God, the reflexive self seeks to understand more profoundly the nature of its own creation and lifelong relationship with God as a being whose days are formed as a book. (Graham, Walton and Ward 2005: 21)

I suggest that this particular interpretation of reflexivity is quite distinct from the ways in which the term is now used within other disciplines and that it is not adequate, particularly when it comes to the discussion about the impact of globalization. The danger of using the concept in this way is not simply that of being excessively individualistic and neglecting the wider context, but of being overly rationalistic. What I mean by this is that it suggests that the individual by using some process or technique of self-reflection, can achieve greater transparency and understanding of himself or herself, in ways that will then lead in a linear fashion to an increased self-awareness and control over one's actions within the world. It becomes a form of cognitive therapy, a 'working upon the self' that can be guaranteed to deepen one's self-understanding.

One might argue that this is an essentially psychologically based concept of reflexivity, whereas the one that I encounter in thinking about globalization is much more sociologically based. Perhaps both are valid in their different spheres. However, in terms of its use within practical theology, this could easily lead to confusion and a clouding of significant differences. Once again I will turn to some of Beck's work in order to illustrate this.

His initial use of the term was as part of his theory of reflexive modernization, but it rapidly led to an internal debate within sociology conducted between himself, Anthony Giddens and Scott Lash (Beck, Giddens and Lash 1994). Without going into the full details of this it becomes clear that what is at stake are both the unconscious dimensions of human operation and the unintended consequences of actions, both of which radically challenge the notion of a linear and cognitive process of increased self-awareness. In his disagreement with Lash in particular, Beck says:

> It is precisely the distinction between cognitive, moral and aesthetic dimensions of reflexive modernization which makes it clear that Lash speaks exclusively of (more or less conscious) reflection, and misunderstands the problematic of unconscious, unintended reflexivity in the sense of self-application, self-dissolution and the self-endangerment of industrial modernization. (Beck, Giddens and Lash 1994: 176)

In contrast to the classic reflection theory of modernity, which argues that the more agents or subjects acquire the ability to reflect on the social conditions of their existence the more they are to be able to change them, this theory of reflexive modernization suggests that there is a process of undermining and destroying the foundations of social and individual existence. This may well be happening without any conscious reflection or explicit knowledge of what is occurring. In other words, modernization in its latest form as globalization is tearing down the traditional structures of social and family life leaving individuals to construct alternatives.

In a later text Beck offers some clear examples of this, ones that are highly relevant to practical theology and its need to understand what is happening in people's lives (Beck and Beck-Gernsheim 2002). He calls this movement 'institutionalized individualism', but again one must be careful not to equate this with individualism as simply self-control and a conscious approach based on human autonomy. It is more like a process which is taking place behind our backs and where we find ourselves forced to construct our own lives from scratch, denied access to the previously secure resources of tradition and social structure. The fact that most of us are now having to play a whole series of different and sometimes conflicting roles in our daily lives – what the sociologists call differentiation – is itself at the root of this problem.

> To the extent that society breaks down into separate functional spheres that are neither interchangeable nor graftable onto one another, people are integrated into society only in their partial aspects as taxpayers, car drivers, students, consumers, voters, patients, producers, fathers, mothers, pedestrians and so on. Constantly changing between different, partly incompatible logics of action, they are forced to take into their hands that which is in danger of breaking to pieces: their own lives. (Beck and Beck-Gernsheim 2002: 23)

So we are forced into creating our own 'do-it-yourself biographies' in a context where the traditional resources of family, religion and even government provision can no longer be leant upon or taken for granted. Each individual has to take responsibility for himself or herself and then live with the consequences. A classic example of this is the choices that parents exercise over their children's education. Make the wrong choice, even in the first few years of a child's life, and they may suffer irrevocably by not gaining access to the right social networks or job opportunities within the highly competitive global economy. The result of this is not a greater self-awareness and control over one's life at all.

> People struggle to live their own lives in a world that increasingly and more evidently escapes their grasp, one that is irrevocably and globally networked … In the global age, one's own life is no longer sedentary or tied to a particular place. It is a travelling life, both literally and metaphorically, a nomadic life, a life spent in cars, aeroplanes and trains, on the telephone or on the internet, supported by the mass media, a transnational life stretching across frontiers. (Beck and Beck-Gernsheim 2002: 25)

Some of these themes will be returned to in later chapters, but it is crucial to grasp from the outset that we are dealing with a very different concept of reflexivity, one which appears to be in sharp contrast to that employed within practical theology. It does not mean a self-conscious pursuit of greater self-awareness that leads to heightened understanding and control over one's life, but processes that are occurring as a result of global change and that undermine the previous structures of social and personal life. One has no choice but to choose how to construct one's life, even though one may not have the necessary resources to do this. This notion of reflexivity is unsettling but surely a more accurate description of the way in which we now live and the pressures we face to be successful.

Conclusion

Having conducted a preliminary survey of the territory, it is becoming clear that the issues encountered under the heading of globalization are more than simply a series of incremental changes to which practical theology must adapt as it takes seriously the context in which it is operating. The impact of globalization is likely to be fundamental and deep rooted, challenging the very frameworks and concepts that are familiar to the practice of Christian ministry. In due course we will examine the areas traditionally attended to by practical theologians: for instance, the geographically bounded nature of local ministry and the sense of place characteristic of much congregational life and development; the nature of pastoral care and community activity and ways in which this is changing; the conduct of worship and its slide towards entertainment and a consumer-based model; the sphere of spirituality itself and the authority – or lack of it – now exercised by tradition and its officials; how work with particular groups, notably young families and young people, is changing; the world of work and how this affects both parochial ministry and other forms of chaplaincy; and issues such as global ethics and the involvement of faith groups in political and social agendas.

What emerges already is that globalization is creating a environment in which people feel overwhelmed by the scale and scope of the changes now under way. Tried and tested means of structuring and organizing our lives are brought into question' and it will not do simply to resort to traditional categories of thought and analysis as responses are formulated. The boundaries are being transgressed and becoming blurred; people feel trapped by the new enclosures created by global capitalism; even attempts to increase self-awareness are being challenged and undermined by forces beyond anybody's control. Fear for the future whether caused by terrorism or concern for environmental disaster create a world in which it is harder to believe that 'business as usual' is a realistic option. Meanwhile the power-brokers of this new age would have us accept that there is no alternative to the onward march of a form of globalization that benefits them, but few of the rest. A critical Christian emancipatory practice needs to show that there are other possibilities, that the thresholds to another world are already in place. The developing resources of practical theology, learning from the insights of other disciplines, will assist in this task.

Chapter 2

A Sense of Place

Introduction

One of the abiding features of the parochial ministry which is central to the concerns of much practical theology is the supposed attachment of people to a sense of place. The commitment over time to a specific geographical locality appears to be essential to the practice and self-understanding of both religion and spirituality. For instance, a recent and well-received book on Christian theology of place suggests that 'one of the best ways in which Christians can witness to the importance of place in all aspects of human experience is by cherishing their holy places' (Inge 2003: 122). The author promotes a sacramental understanding of place and believes that churches can become shrines which speak to others of God's presence in the midst of a secular world.

> Should not all churches be places wherein there is a history of divine self-communication, of 'sacramental encounters' with the worshipping community that inhabits them? Should not their presence in the midst of that community nourish the faith of that community? Should they not proclaim to the secular world in which they stand that God is present and active in the world? Cannot each journey made to such a church be thought of as a 'mini-pilgrimage'? In short, should not every church be understood as a shrine? (Inge 2003: 115)

The approach of this chapter is to suggest that such a sacramental understanding of ordinary congregations towards their church buildings already exists, but that the problem is that the changed context in which the tradition now operates means that the possibilities of this practice meaning anything to those outside church boundaries are strictly limited. Here is another zombie category where it is still possible to interpret current practice in a traditional manner without realizing that even regular church-goers may now see their relationship to a particular place in more fluid and complex ways.

Even at the point where the parish system in the Anglican Church could be interpreted as being at breaking point with staffing levels and financial support unable to sustain a pattern of ordained presence in single parishes, the underlying supposition is still that this relationship between people and a specific building is the ideal configuration. How can the necessary relationship between priest and people develop unless there is continuity of contact between the two within the confines of a manageable area? In the various reorganizations that are the response to the current staffing crisis in the rural church, for instance, the question is still to how wide an area or to how many different communities a priest can minister effectively. If it is no longer possible to provide enough stipendiary clergy to service this system then the alternative is to find other forms of ministry, local non-stipendiary or lay, that will enable the geographically based pattern to survive.

Other denominations have apparently abandoned the attempt to retain this type of coverage and instead explicitly minister to gathered congregations focusing on centres of population and expecting their people to travel in. However, there is still an identifiable geographical centre and an identifiable area to which the minister relates and to which their people are deemed to belong. This is more than a matter of pure convenience, it is also to do with identity and a sense of belonging.

Beyond the strictly religious culture the questions 'where do you come from' or 'where do you live', still have a significant impact. But are such views of the relationship between place and identity not being changed or undermined by the dynamics of globalization? If it is the case that boundaries are becoming blurred, that increasing numbers of people feel constrained or enclosed by the difficulties of not being able to travel or by being forced to travel constantly by their work or other circumstances, and that we are aware of our locations in new and reflexive ways, then is this not going to have an effect upon practical theology?

A few examples might illuminate this. In what ways are boundaries being blurred? Some more affluent families not only have second homes in this country, but also properties in Portugal or Spain if not further afield. Which one is their 'home'? Some will spend six months in one house and six in the other. What constitutes home in any case? They may get involved in this country when they are here and even be church-goers, but how does this dual or multiple residency impact upon the nature of that involvement? Then there are the many commuters who decide where to live on the basis of access to motorways or airports but have no intention of 'putting down roots' or engaging in any local activity. What is home to them other than a base from which they travel and commute? It is possibly somewhere for family to reside while the children undergo schooling, but even that may happen elsewhere and not in the immediate locality. Some of the terms that are now being used by sociologists to describe this are 'tourists', in the sense that people are always on the move and consuming different places rather than dwelling in them (Bauman 1993: 240), or 'vagabonds', to portray the restless and rootless nature of this existence. Within religious traditions there is the concept of pilgrimage of course, but how might this relate to these new patterns of living? A vagabond is a pilgrim without a destination perhaps?

Under what circumstances is an attachment to a particular locality either an enclosure or a threshold? One might recall the petrol-delivery strikes in the UK of a few years ago when suddenly those living in rural areas and some distance from potential sources of fuel were stranded and unable to drive their cars. They felt trapped and cut off from the rest of life very rapidly. The inability to drive felt like a loss of freedom and a deprivation of normal activity. On the other hand there are many people who have no choice but to drive long distances on a regular basis in order to fulfil their working commitments and may also feel trapped stuck in long tailbacks on the motorways. They might argue that this is necessary in order to pay the mortgage so that they can reside in their chosen location and participate in a sense of place in another part of their lives.

It is now unusual to encounter people who have been born and lived in the same house for the whole of their lives, but it does still happen. Is their sense of place different from those who have moved around? Does this affect their understanding of religion in any way? One might imagine that people now move around more than was ever the case in the past, but it would be a mistake to assume that mobility is a recent phenomenon. Waves of people migrated to other parts of the UK at various stages over the last three centuries, often determined by the search for employment or because of family commitments. The BBC TV programme *Who do You Think You Are?*, which helps personalities track their own family history, has been very revealing and illustrated the extent to which quite ordinary families had moved and been prepared to abandon their roots to make a fresh start elsewhere. There is also a UK university website which has tracked the most common family names through the census data from 1881 onwards in order to show in which parts of the country these names were most evident and how that has changed over the last 100 years. Many will have been concentrated within limited geographical areas in the nineteenth century but have since become dispersed.

So how important are the ties to locality? Are they changing as lifestyles become more fluid and access to travel that much easier? One might take the opportunity to encourage people to reflect upon their sense of place and the nature of their commitment to locality and community. Even though there have been times when clergy have remained in a particular post for many years, and thus remained a solid point of reference and constant presence, this is now the exception rather than the rule and probably viewed with disfavour by both parish clergy themselves and the ecclesiastical hierarchy. It was more likely to happen when communities were themselves more static. It contrasts with the understanding that, as a minister, one does not belong anywhere, but expects either to be moved or to move around as one's location is dependent upon one's work and calling. It seems that this, in itself, represents a change in perceptions that could well be a result of the greater mobility and insecurity that people feel as a consequence. As their lives are less stable and more likely to change, so they are more likely to project onto the minister the very stability and sense of belonging to a place which they crave and idealize because it contrasts with their own experience. Their sense of wanting to belong becomes displaced onto the 'local professional', who then represents that appearance of continuity and stability.

Whether one can then assist people in reflecting upon this is another matter, as they are probably not aware of, nor would not want to be reminded of, the lack of stability in their own lives. These are the sort of changes which happen 'behind our backs' or are forced upon us by circumstances over which we may feel we have little control – employment prospects and family break-ups are two obvious examples of this. But this does illustrate the complexity of analysing the importance of a sense of place and indeed of how this relates to religious life and the development of commitment and a contemporary spirituality.

Local Church as Faithful Spaces

Most recent writing on the theme of how traditional religion relates to a sense of place and the importance of locality tends to re-emphasize a conservative view of these matters. It is assumed that attachment to a building or even a churchyard is of psychological significance and that this remains constant despite other cultural shifts. Two examples of this are a workbook on rural ministry (Hopkinson 2005) and the report *Faithful Cities* (Commission on Urban Life and Faith 2006), which was a return to some of the issues raised by *Faith in the City* published in 1985.

Turning first to the rural dimension, the workbook argues that people require a greater sense of locality given the rapidly changing pace of contemporary life:

> In an increasingly busy and fast changing society, people often need to have roots, a sense of memories held in trust and a sense of continuity. In rural communities, that sense of place, and the faithful worship, even by only a few people, can have significance well beyond the church walls … for some people, their own walk with God is especially supported by the knowledge that prayer and worship is taking place within their locality … [this] sustains others in their lives and work, whether that be a prosperous local business or the intense hardship of events like the foot-and-mouth outbreak. (Hopkins 2005: 11)

It is also argued that the church building is often a focus for other local activity, providing a meeting place for social events and even being used for a Post Office or other commercial purposes. This is almost a return to the Middle Ages when both church and churchyard were a centre for village life, and fairs and community events took place in both locations since these were indeed public spaces.

A concern with these claims is that there is both an element of confusion and also an unwillingness to recognize that the changes that might once again provide a role for the local church as a building are the very ones that continue to challenge and undermine the attachment to place that is being taken for granted. The only reason for church buildings being used by other facilities is because of political decisions about the withdrawal of services, and that in itself is a symptom of the urbanization of rural life and the fact that many rural dwellers can now travel out of the immediate area for their requirements. It could be argued that using churches for non-ecclesiastical activity is only for the benefit of those who have been left behind by the changing nature of rural life, such as the local elderly and young families with limited transport options. Quite how sustainable such projects are likely to be is therefore an open question. I would suggest that this has little to do with any real attachment to place.

The deeper question which these claims fail to address is that of how the nature of the attachment to place equates with the continued importance of a local worshipping community. There is no doubt that in times of collective and personal crisis, such as the 2001 foot-and-mouth outbreak in the UK, a level of reassurance and pastoral care was available because of the existence of the parish system in its various forms. But, in fact, because farms were placed under restriction orders the main means of outside contact was by telephone. Much pastoral work done by clergy and laity at this time did not take place face-to-face, even though it may have developed relationships which had been established in that way.

It is also true that the continued presence of a local church and minister is significant when it comes to the occasional offices (baptisms, weddings and funerals) and the reassuring presence during personal trauma or rites of passage. However, the acts of worship now being constructed around those events are themselves being influenced and shaped by global cultural change. For instance, increasing numbers of clergy handle draft wedding services through e-mail attachment following an initial interview with the couple, often because one or both are located elsewhere in the country or even in the world. Many weddings are of daughters coming home to their parent's location because that is where they still have emotional ties, but there is very little likelihood of further pastoral contact apart from visits home on special occasions. There is nothing wrong with this, but it does represent the greater mobility now characteristic of a global society.

The other thing to note is the way in which couples for weddings, and even families for baptisms and funerals, now access material from the internet in order to construct their own personalized service for these occasions. This is not a manifestation of the 'good old days' when everybody lived together in tight-knit communities and shared social and personal life, but rather a matter of creating identity from the fragmented components available in a global culture, some of which are still related to a particular place and a specific personal history. Practical theology is in danger of being based on zombie categories if it assumes that nothing has changed. Things appear to be the same because the elements being employed are the same, but the ways in which they are being employed are subtly and importantly different and this is the result of changes in the social and cultural context.

These changes are less easy to disguise in an urban setting and so, as one might expect, the *Faithful Cities* report is somewhat more explicit about the changing role of religious activity. This is in the context of discussions about what constitutes a 'good city' and builds upon a more fluid model of social engagement. Hence:

> The only future for cities is a sustainable future. The theme of restlessness – of journey and migration – can be helpful here. Cities tend to see themselves as monoliths over against 'the country', whereas, in fact, in order to work they rely upon sophisticated networks of distribution and exchange. Cities are re-made every day. (Commission on Urban Life and Faith 2006: 56)

The report goes on to suggest that this can be mirrored by the nature of the Christian community, particularly as it learns to work alongside other faith groupings and to acknowledge the existence of a wider range of sacred space:

> The ability to respond to these diverse needs for sacred space is an indicator of a city and its residents' well-being. Again, for Christianity, this theme of restlessness is important. Christian communities need places to perform their rituals but don't need to command or control space. Religious communities must not mirror the turf wars between developers, by engaging in battles over sacred space. (Commission on Urban Life and Faith 2006: 57)

However, despite this more enlightened approach to the importance of place and locality, the report does then go on to emphasize the role of specific buildings very much along the lines of its rural counterpart. It argues that as well as having a symbolic presence, a church building might be the last remaining communal space within a neighbourhood and therefore of wider community value. What lies behind this is a possible link with the growing government agenda on cohesive communities and sustainable neighbourhoods.

> People of faith increasingly show exceptional commitment to neighbourhoods that experience multiple deprivation and the thousands of local faith-based initiatives are practical responses to the pressures that cities experience in a globalized world. (Commission on Urban Life and Faith 2006: 76)

So there is a greater willingness from within the urban setting to acknowledge that the significance of a sense of place within religious activity is itself part of the social and cultural changes created by globalization, but there is still an attachment to buildings and locality that fails to fully grasp the nature and scope of those changes. Will forms of religious expression themselves be changed by global forces as places become more fluid and self-consciously constructed? I would suggest that we are only at the beginning of answering this question.

The Meaning of Place

The academic study of this subject makes it clear that the concept of place is both complex and contested. Geography as a specialized subject area is the main resource, but this also takes us into the other disciplines of economics, sociology, politics and psychology. The starting point is to recognize that any sense of place is a social construction – there is no such thing as 'place' unless or until somebody has a reason for identifying a particular locality as such. One then encounters the variety of motivations for making that identification which include the possibility that one lives or dwells in a specific location: that one works there, so the relationship with place is primarily economic; that one relates to a group of people who also happen to live in that locality or share its social life in some way, hence the interest is broadly sociological; that a specific place becomes a base for a form of political activity, for instance through a parish or district council. Practical theology tends to trade-off the more overtly psychological dimension of place in that it relates to the construction of a sense of identity – one somehow belongs or is part of a place in a way that offers meaning and direction to one's life. Attachment is seen as essential to knowing who one is both in one's relationship to others but also in relation to God. So how is one to define place? It is:

> A portion of geographic space. Space is organised into places often thought of as bounded settings in which social relations and identity are constituted. Such places may be officially recognised geographical entities or more informally organised sites of intersecting social relations, meanings and collective memory. The concept of place, the uniqueness of particular places and place-based identities are hotly contested concepts in the contemporary context of increasing globalization and the perceived threat of growing placelessness. (Johnston et al. 2000: 582)

It is clear that globalization has impinged upon the understanding of place according to the discipline of geography, but in what way? The sense that people are becoming increasingly rootless and no longer significantly attached to specific localities can create a form of nostalgia and attempts to construct an idealized past based on being embedded and belonging. The 'myth of community', a time when people knew everybody else in their immediate locality and shared common interests and values, has an understandable attraction.

A danger for churches and congregations in this context is that they readily buy into and encourage this myth as it appears to coincide with a time when their hold over people was stronger and when the local church was 'at the heart of the community'. The image of the church alongside the village green with people flocking through its doors to worship and celebrate together is a powerful one, but hardly represents life as it was even in the time when every parish had its own minister. It ignores the extent to which the Church of England in particular was closely identified with the upper echelons of rural society and relied upon a position of privilege and power to sustain its role in what was a largely agricultural and hierarchically structured society. Yet this picture is still presented as an ideal for rural ministry, and clergy and laity are encouraged to recreate this enclosed and static social structure in order to foster traditional values and a return to the 'good old days', when squire and parson stood shoulder to shoulder at the centre of a stable community.

What most geographers present is a much more fluid and complex image of locality and place. Variety, diversity and difference are the consequences of global forces upon most if not all communities. People increasingly relate to others across the country and across the globe through better communications and are not restricted to contact with those in the immediate locality. One can easily live in a rural area, for instance, and choose not to encounter those who live nearby or to participate in any local activities. One of the constant complaints of rural congregations who represent the longer-standing inhabitants of an area is that newcomers move in and do not get involved, thus reproducing the suburban social patterns that they may claim to have left behind, but in reality they transplant them to these more spacious and pleasant surroundings. Geographer Doreen Massey presents the idea of a progressive concept of place. This recognizes the open and porous boundaries of places as well as the myriad interlinkages and interdependencies between them. It also assumes social and cultural heterogeneity within places rather than assimilation to a national or local norm:

> Any given place is materially and imaginatively constructed by many different types of people. The dynamic tension created by the co-presence of all these people results in each lending different dimensions to those places. (Massey, quoted in Johnston et al. 2000: 583)

In terms of our central concerns one can see that the issue of blurring of boundaries results from this process and that one must raise the question of whether certain communities are enclosures or thresholds to other possibilities. The time when places were close-knit and enclosed were surely constraining for those who did not have the resources to venture far beyond their immediate locality, while the more affluent had the monopoly of opportunities to travel and broaden their horizons. The encounter with the urban or the cities of the time were the thresholds to other worlds, whereas now this is more likely to be the role of global travel and communications.

Another related argument is that globalization creates homogeneity and a standardization of both place and culture, thus destroying real differences. For instance, there are suggestions that shopping malls and supermarkets are driving High Street shops out of business and creating a monochrome town and city environment. Places are becoming the same in appearance and character because of the regularizing impact of multinational companies and the large retail outlets. How can places retain their individuality and distinctive character? Church buildings and their related communities might appear to be a bastion against this type of invasion, a means by which a locality can retain its own culture. But is this any more than a romantic reaction against the supposed appropriation of the local by the global and, even if it does have some reality to it, is it a legitimate role for faith groups to play? Are faith communities supposed to be groupings of those who clearly share common values and interests or are they supposed rather to be open to difference and able to welcome and provide hospitality to strangers and those who are 'other'? This is surely a fundamental theological question which must have an impact upon our view of the importance of place and ways in which that might now be changing.

Questions for Practical Theology

Before moving on to examine some resources from the discipline of political sociology, let us articulate the questions which are starting to emerge from this study. It is not obvious what exactly constitutes or creates a sense of place. Is it simply related to a specific geographical locality? Is this, in itself, more about personal history, about relationships or local involvement or association with one's key life events? What does this mean, now that many people's lives are more mobile and it is possible that they reside in a number of locations over time or even at the same time? It is also likely that those who participate in the global culture will see residence in the same place for a long time as a way of being trapped or enclosed, a failure to move on and progress in one's working or social life. So spaces are as likely to be perceived as zones of restriction as they are as places of security and stability. They might also become places of conflict where those who have the capacity to move around, reside for a while, consume what they desire and then move on, while those who have no choice but to remain lose out in terms of resources and facilities.

Then one needs to be aware of the interests behind the definitions of place. Who sets city and parish boundaries and what lies behind those decisions? What happens when church boundaries do not coincide with the civil boundaries, let alone when it comes to drawing up new boundaries of parishes and groups? External authorities setting the definitions of places often complicate and disturb existing senses of place. For instance, neighbouring villages which have lived in a state of tension dating back to the English Civil War have been put in new parish teams by diocesan decisions, or villages that look in different directions because of school or shopping facilities are also sometimes placed together to the frustration of local people and clergy. One cannot separate definitions of place from the exercise of power.

A further problem is to identify precisely what is meant by belonging to a particular community or locality. Is it enough simply to reside in a location, or does one need to have either a historic connection or else to participate in some way in existing local activities? There can be both the subjective dimension of feeling that one belongs and also the more objective level of being accepted by others, and then there is the legal level of being on an electors register or on a roll for church membership. The question of who is a genuine local can arise when it comes to allocating housing for local people in a Housing Association development. How long does one have to have lived in a place before one is counted as a local?

Beyond this is the troubled issue of identity itself and this is where the disciplines of philosophy and psychology have insights to offer. Is there such a thing as one's 'core identity' and, if so, how is this constructed? What role does a sense of place play in this process? If most people are now more mobile and move from place to place because of work opportunities, are they not capable of rebuilding and changing their sense of themselves in ways that relate far less to specific locations? It is not unusual to encounter families or individuals who have been church-goers or supporters in one place but then lapse completely when they relocate, either because they no longer want to exercise that level of commitment or because they do not feel 'at home' with the new congregation or minister. What other factors now play a part in how one constructs one's sense of self? One might suggest that attachment to place is only one of a number of possible components upon which people draw in order to create their identity. It is one resource amongst many and perhaps a less significant one in these times of greater mobility, in which case, what are the implications of this for the shape and self-understanding of pastoral ministry and practical theology?

Exploring Distant Proximities

This subject area is both complex and confusing, and it is difficult to reach clear conclusions about the changing relationship between the local and the global and how this is impacting upon the traditional concerns of practical theology. A problem is the lack of a convincing framework of explanation for the experiences one encounters. The work of the political sociologist James Rosenau *Distant Proximities* (2003) is helpful in this respect.

'Distant proximities' is the phrase Rosenau employs to describe the tension that is a constant feature of this new configuration. He argues that the world is now integrating and disintegrating at the same time. What seems remote can also appear close at hand, and what might seem distant can be immediate and powerfully present. The very term 'globalization' cannot adequately describe this experience. A secure grasp of world affairs requires that one carefully examines these distant proximities.

> One discovers quickly that distant proximities are not simple interrelationships, readily discernable and easily understood. [They] encompass the tensions between core and periphery, between national and transnational systems, between communitarianism and cosmopolitanism, between cultures and subcultures, between states and markets, between urban and rural, between coherence and incoherence, between integration and

> disintegration, between centralization and decentralization … between pace and space, between global and local. (Rosenau 2003: 4–5)

How one experiences these tensions depends upon where one is located in the world, not just in terms of geography but also in terms of employment, politics and culture. So there is a huge diversity of experience and responses to the forces currently at work. There is also a considerable subjective element to such responses hence the difficulty of emerging with any objective measurements of what is happening. What one does need to guard against is the simplistic judgement that global = bad, while local = good. One must also beware of assuming that globalization automatically leads to fragmentation while localism is to be equated with integration. The complexity encountered leads Rosenau to coin the term 'fragmegration' – a hybrid word that expresses the confusion of possibilities (2003: 11). He supports the observation that some people experience greater mobility and flexibility as a positive result of global changes while others are threatened and disturbed by them. Some are unsettled once they realize that they have to take greater responsibility for constructing their own lives and their own identity and can no longer fall back upon the resources of tradition and culture to create an unquestioning structure. Others however see this as liberating and exciting. Protest movements against globalization may be the result of resistance to psychological as well as to economic upheaval.

Local Worlds

One of the most helpful parts of Rosenau's work for practical theology is his categorization of different approaches to global change made at a local level. Whilst acknowledging that there is a plethora of local worlds, and that any attempt at providing neat divisions is limited, he also argues that it is possible to identify distinct differences between different groupings and this enables us to highlight some of the issues already encountered.

> Just as it is impossible to draw clear-cut lines between the local and the global, since these concepts embrace mental constructs as well as geographical spaces, so it is difficult to delineate unmistakeable boundaries that separate the various local worlds ... To depict the emergent epoch as consisting of four local, four global, and four private worlds is to draw a picture that is ... 'highly simplified' ... Yet if we are to think seriously about the world, and act effectively in it, some sort of simplified map of reality, some theory, concept, model, paradigm is necessary. (Rosenau 2003: 80)

As long one is aware of the limitations of this exercise it can still be of benefit. Rosenau describes four types of local worlds: Insular Locals; Resistant Locals; Exclusionary Locals and Affirmative Locals. He suggests that globalizing dynamics are boundary-blurring while localizing dynamics tend to be boundary-affirming, so it is best to ignore the national dimension of these movements and to concentrate instead on a much more local awareness.

> If globalization is a matter of increasing long-distance interconnectedness, at least across national boundaries, preferably between continents as well, then localization involves

> processes wherein connections within countries are either reduced to, preserved by, or confined to existing or smaller jurisdictions, preferably within subnational spaces or even subprovincial spaces but not excluding national spaces. (Rosenau 2003: 85)

One of the problems with this discussion is that of pitching the analysis at the appropriate level and there is a significant debate about the role of the nation and the nation state within the processes of globalization. Let us see whether or not one can recognize the different types of local that Rosenau presents.

First of all he suggests that Insular Locals tend to live in enclosed communities, Resistant Locals will operate in political arenas, Exclusionary Locals will live in deliberate enclaves, but Affirmative Locals will live in open communities. So 'Insulars' will have historic ties to specific geographical areas and probably remain remote from much global change. 'Resistants' will object to the destabilization of traditional and familiar patterns of life encountered in a globalizing world. 'Exclusionaries' choose to cut themselves off from these changes because they are perceived to be threatening to their sense of identity, possibly based on ethnic origins. 'Affirmatives' still value the role of the local but have come to terms with the changes and distant proximities that are an inevitable consequence of globalization (Rosenau 2003: 91).

One can begin to see immediately how different groups and individuals fit these categories and where church congregations might be close to a particular approach. How likely is it that there will be many 'Insulars' around any longer in the UK, Western Europe or the USA, since most people have now been affected by the processes of global change? The point is that they might not otherwise have been aware that such things were happening because of their geographical or cultural remoteness. There may be some 'Resistants' in areas that are on the edges of these changes and are just beginning to feel the impact upon their way of life. So perhaps some remoter rural areas now affected by people moving in from outside or commuting long distances to work would be aware that this is part of a more significant process of change that might threaten the accepted patterns of locality and culture. 'Locals versus newcomers' debates are not unknown still in smaller communities and the problem of lack of affordable housing for local people could be seen as an aspect of this (Reader 2005).

Whether church congregations and worshippers fall into the 'Exclusionary' category, deliberately pulling up the drawbridge and attempting to create new enclosed communities that resist global change is an important question. I would suggest that moves to construct tight-knit or socially monochrome groupings centred on a church or worship base might well fit this description in some cases. The real issue is the openness of such groups, both to those who are different from themselves and to the practical changes in life and lifestyle created by globalization. Self-consciously constructing clear and identifiable boundaries in order to decide who is 'inside' and who is 'outside' seems to be just such a process and could well be a reaction against the blurring and confusion created by global change.

It looks as though the 'Affirmatives' might have some sort of greater credibility and a more realistic approach to what is happening around them, but even this is not so clear-cut. They might be in danger of compromising or losing something distinctive and central to their culture or values by readily accepting the changes. How much is lost in the process of adaptation and might this include some elements vital to maintaining Christian belief and tradition?

It is interesting to see where Rosenau himself places people within this spectrum. For a start he sees church groups as sitting within the category of Insular Locals:

> The spatially proximate community of the Insular Local includes the neighbourhood as a specific territory, the family as a hearth, the church as a haven, the school as a place of learning, the job as a place of employment, and the nearby store as a place to shop and socialize. They are all, as it were, located at particular addresses … All of them are nearby; they have clear-cut boundaries; they can be visited easily; their meaning is normally clear and uncomplicated; they help people define who they are and what they want. (Rosenau 2003: 92–3)

Both a sense of identity and a sense of place are determined by that which is close at hand and immediate in time and space. Other aspects of community life will be recognizable within this configuration, for instance participation in local social and political activities. Although there may be an awareness that decisions made beyond the immediate locality impinge upon local affairs, the concentration is still upon the local impact of such decisions. Much of this resonates with the image of church life in smaller, rural communities and certainly the vision of what community life should be like, even if it is not. But how realistic is this?

Rosenau himself says that, in some respects, this world is a myth: 'or at least the notion of a neighbourhood community wherein people know each other, attend the same meetings, share occupational concerns, talk across fences, and subscribe to the same values can be readily exaggerated' (Rosenau 2003: 95). It sounds like the outsider's view of small-town America or of idealized village life in the UK. Such images invariably disguise levels of conflict and disharmony that are hidden from the outsider in any case, as people do not like to admit what really happens within such closely contained communities. The problem for church and congregational life, even in some suburban areas, is that it wants to 'live the dream' or trade-off the illusion that this accurately represents the sort of relationships that are fostered by religious values. But if much of this is either a myth or an illusion, then what is the reality in a globalized world and have Christian groups come to terms with this and the possibility that it is another zombie category?

Might religious groups fit more readily and appropriately into one of the other categories? The answer is not straightforward. Resistant Locals might appear to be people who oppose the effects of globalization upon their own employment prospects or lifestyle, but they might also be concerned about the homogenization of local cultures or the threat to the local ecosystem posed by rapid industrialization. There can be legitimate collective and individual motives for placing oneself in this category. It is also possible that they might decide to engage in global matters in order to fight for or to protect what they consider to be of value at local level: 'for Resistant Locals, the scalar boundaries of the local are variable as they strive to prevent the impact of unwanted distant proximities' (Rosenau 2003: 98). Some of the anti-globalization demonstrations of recent years probably represent such an approach and these have included people of faith concerned about the impact of globalization not only upon themselves but also upon other vulnerable groups. So it is to be expected that one might find Christians within this grouping of Resistant Locals.

What about the world of the Exclusionary Locals? For them the local is seen as a refuge, retreat or safe space protected from the ravages of global change and they may be seeking some sort of counter-cultural movement based upon a return to the practices and values of locality.

> However, these intellectually driven Exclusionary Locals are small in number compared with those whose emotional needs for identity with and support for others sharing the same heritage lead them to seek exclusion behind the walls of ethnicity, nationality, religion, language, or whatever common links to others may bring psychic security. (Rosenau 2003: 106)

The bonds created by belonging to a specific religious tradition might easily allow people to become Exclusionary Locals, seeking a safe haven against the external threats posed by the cultural and political impact of global change, itself perhaps identified with Westernization or Americanization. Ethnicity or religious affiliation will themselves be constructs, but this does not make them any less significant or effective, if protest and resistance is what is required. Nationalism can become a form of localism in this context if it is used to try to set clear and secure boundaries against the 'other'. 'Exclusionary Locals seek to render inconsequential the dynamics of globalization by closing themselves off from the intrusions of a globalizing world' (Rosenau 2003: 107).

Having said all of that, and acknowledged that people of faith are to be found in each of the foregoing categories, it is most likely that many Christians will be Affirmative Locals according to Rosenau's definition. These are people who both recognize the scale and scope of global change and are also prepared to adapt to it and are comfortable in doing so. Immediate personal benefit may be a critical factor, but they might see that others are likely to share in these improvements and in expanded horizons and possibilities. So it is not that the local no longer matters, but rather that there are as likely to be gains from the changes as there are losses and that it is possible to harness these for both collective and individual benefit. The potential threats are outweighed by the opportunities and, since change is a natural part of life, things have to move on and adapt in order to survive. This is not pure pragmatism but can be based upon principled interpretations of the nature of the processes set in train by globalization, not made in an uncritical fashion but being aware of the possible dangers. I suspect that many church-goers would feel comfortable with this category, even though they might sometimes like to claim they are being counter-cultural and would prefer to set tight and secure boundaries.

The questions for those of faith are those of where they should stand and of what judgements they should be passing upon the impact of globalization. What emphasis should they place upon the local? At this point one might conclude that any stance entails certain ambiguities and complexities and that no one of Rosenau's categories presents itself as the sole approach to follow. What the argument suggests is that Christians need to be more aware of these complexities and of the dangers of adopting what might appear to be a traditional approach. The myth of the local and the temptation to try to draw clear and sharp boundaries needs to be interpreted in this light.

Place and Identity

I have been arguing that the disciplines of geography and political sociology can assist practical theology in understanding how the significance of place has changed with the impact of globalization. One interpretation that needs to be resisted is that place is no longer significant in the process of identity construction. Such a view is not supported by the evidence. However, neither does it appear to be the case that a sense of place continues to contribute to the creation of a sense of self and indeed of social relationships in the same way as before. Greater mobility, fluidity and constant crossing of previously clear and identifiable boundaries add levels of complexity and confusion that raise the question of how exactly place plays a role in the way that we view and interpret our lives. Given that attachment to locality has been such an important factor in the formation of congregational life and of personal spirituality, practical theology needs to take note of these changes.

At the heart of this debate is the issue of whether or not human beings construct a solid and unchanging sense of themselves, particularly in the light of the boundary-blurring processes associated with globalization. To refer once again to Rosenau, he argues that this is definitely no longer the case:

> Increasingly people have to think of themselves in terms of a multiplicity of identities … gone are the days when one could define oneself in terms of a singular geographic space. In large part due to dynamic technologies, there has been a 'dissolution of self', a fragmenting of interests, values and affiliations such that the individual has different identities that can vary as widely as the different interests, values and affiliations one might have. (Rosenau 2003: 181)

Instead of one clear and constant sense of self, there is more likely to be a proliferation of identities as one's expanse of relationships and contacts widens, sometimes on a daily basis. Saying who you are, where you come from, what work you do and where your family resides, are no longer guaranteed means of capturing one's sense of self, although they are still of importance. Most people will feel that they are based somewhere and that there is one location that they consider to be home. Without that one might feel oneself to be a refugee, vagabond or nomad of some sort, lacking the psychic security that is essential to a stable personal or communal existence. Yet this can shade into a multiplicity of possibilities and a sense that one has to be a different person in different locations in differing sets of relationships, and this in a way that is about more than playing different roles. Perhaps, as Rosenau says, this is fragmegration, a simultaneous process of integrating and disintegrating, as circumstances dictate. The capacity to learn and adapt is crucial and that process will draw upon the resources one has in creating a changing identity. One of those resources may well be a sense of place. Another may also be a sense of oneself as a person of faith. Whether either can now wholly determine who one perceives oneself to be is an important question.

A helpful phrase used by some geographers is 'sticky places and slippery spaces' (Castree et al. 2004: 79). There are places which are still significant in how we see ourselves and our relationships with others, not simply in terms of historic connections and associations, but also in terms of the present. So a local church and congregational life might well be one of those 'sticky places' to which one returns, even though most of one's life is now lived elsewhere. This needs to be respected and honoured by clergy and the institutional church in matters of pastoral care and the occasional offices. But just because somewhere is one of those 'sticky places' one cannot assume that it will translate readily into a deeper form of commitment and attachment to that locality. Alongside that form of attachment to place goes the relationship with many 'slippery spaces' that now also constitutes normal life. 'Slippery spaces' are those locations one encounters perhaps only once, or, at best, irregularly, and yet which can still figure significantly in one's life. Here the bonds are weaker and more fragile and less likely to result in long-term commitment or connection. Yet there could well be far more of these than of the 'sticky places' more often associated with church attendance and affiliation.

If this is indeed the case, then is the role of the local church to create or provide the 'sticky places' that will hold people's attention and energy over time, or perhaps to acknowledge the growing significance of 'slippery spaces' and to be content also to play that role in people's lives? It does not have to be an 'either/or'. It may be possible to do both and indeed appropriate to do so depending on the circumstances. But this will have an impact upon the conduct of worship, the exercise of pastoral care and indeed understandings of personal and collective spirituality. One is both providing the familiar surroundings and elements of a 'sticky places' practical theology but also of a 'slippery spaces' version, where complexity and boundary-blurring activities are perfectly acceptable. The challenge is how to sustain enough support for the 'sticky places' so that they are still there to be accessed by those who would rather encounter them as 'slippery spaces'. For the moment it can be seen that globalization and its study through social science disciplines is illuminating and leads one to question some of the zombie categories of practical theology.

Chapter 3

Pastoral Care and Globalization

Introduction

Pastoral care is undergoing significant changes. Evidence for that is to be found not only in changing patterns of pastoral practice but also in the academic literature on the subject. I take as my starting point Elaine Graham's *Transforming Practice* (Graham 1996), one of the best reinterpretations of what is going on in the field. A number of recent developments have reshaped what is now to be encountered. Put succinctly they are the influences of studies of gender, pluralism, disestablishment and postmodernity. (Graham 1996: 59) I will argue in this chapter that globalization also needs to be on this list, but there are clearly significant overlaps and connections with Graham's other candidates and she herself acknowledges this in her later work (2002: 163–5). Let us first though plot out the territory using her research.

One-to-one individual care has been brought into question, not only because of the practical problems now faced by ministers in terms of time and resources, but also because of theological considerations. What is the purpose of such an activity and who should exercise it? While considerable attention has been given to the development of this into pastoral counselling, the questions raised apply to its wider application in older patterns of individual pastoral encounter. This may not yet be reflected in the day-to-day practice of ministry where certainly many older people will complain that 'the vicar never visits any longer'. Such a response would treat theoretical arguments against the practice as simply an excuse for laziness and neglect.

There are however important issues at stake about the dangers of creating a culture of dependency and also about the exercise of power and control over others. One-to-one pastoral visiting – a somewhat dangerous occupation given recommendations about good pastoral practice which suggest that people of the opposite gender should not be alone together – could be seen as the most effective way of taking an interest in somebody's life and building the relationships vital for parochial ministry. Yet it is clear that there are other ways of achieving these objectives and that such care does not have to be exercised exclusively by an ordained person. I have referred elsewhere (Reader 2005) to the importance of identifying 'locations for encounter' which are just as likely to be collective as they are individual. There are also very practical questions of who is going to be around during the daytime for clergy to visit. Rapidly disappearing are the days when the vicar could wander around his parish and expect to either bump into people, or else drop in on somebody with the likelihood that they would be there waiting for a visit. With most couples both at work, given the pressures of the global economy, and even younger families and older people now much more mobile and less likely to stay behind closed doors during the day unless they are forced to do so, this method of pastoral encounter is increasingly ineffective. With supposedly old-fashioned pastoral visiting, the best way of guaranteeing finding someone at home is by making an appointment in advance.

Even if this method were still of general use, the terms and conditions of the relationship thus established are under question. Problems of the potential abuse of power in such relationships have come to dominate the discussions. This goes beyond the familiar comment of parishioners that 'the minister only calls when he/she wants something'. As Graham says:

> The potential for the abuse of power in the therapeutic relationship has become a matter for concern in recent years … Contemporary writers thus seek a greater equality in the pastoral encounter, arguing that the dynamics of power and difference (of gender, race, class, sexuality and professionalism) need to be addressed honestly and openly. The emphasis is on the mutuality of care in contrast to the formality and hierarchy of old. (Graham 1996: 49)

This does not mean that one-to-one visiting is necessarily inappropriate, but rather that certain crucial considerations have to be thought through before this approach is adopted. One is obviously the vulnerability of both parties given the particular situation. But it is undoubtedly true that innocence has been lost from this means of pastoral encounter.

A further dimension relates to the context of a greater cultural pluralism and thus the authority – or lack of it – that any representative of a specific religious tradition might hold in such encounters. Thus, for instance, even when dealing with the rites of passage – bereavements, weddings, baptisms – there is no guarantee that the parties involved will have any religious commitment or share the values and beliefs of the minister or lay person making the contact. In which case the whole dynamic of the relationship is different and the question of the meaning and purpose of this liturgy to the person requesting it cannot be presupposed.

What is the starting point of the religious representative most likely to be, and how might this cohere with the expectations and requirements of the other person? If, for instance, the former is coming from a basically liberal humanist perspective grounded in the familiar values of a belief in human progress, and thus also adopting a non-judgemental or non-directive approach, then there is no guarantee that this will be shared.

> Thus the ultimate goal of the modern pastoral care movement has been one of personal wholeness and well-being; but the individual is seen as possessing an innate orientation towards such self-actualization. Certainly, there is some concession to moral judgement in the form of confrontation in the counselling relationship; but this seems orientated more towards encouragement of ethical autonomy than obedience to external moral codes. (Graham 1996: 50)

Hence there is both an internal question for Christian pastoral practice about its own moral discourse and also an external one about the multiplicity of values likely to be encountered in a society inhabited by a wide variety of people from differing traditions.

A further symptom of the changing nature of pastoral care is the growing concern for the social and political dimensions of the discipline. It is well established that caring for people also requires an awareness of and a willingness to respond to the wider determinants of their lives. Writing from within a background in industrial chaplaincy as well as parochial ministry, I would argue very strongly that pastoral care is so much more than the 'plaster and bandages' approach of simply standing alongside individuals at times of need. That is still a legitimate and important dimension of the task. But, for instance, if it is clear that the root cause of an individual's problems lies in the relationships and demands of their workplace and that there are structural and institutional ills that need to be addressed, then it is part of the task of pastoral ministry to bring those to the surface. This applies equally to wider questions of justice both within and between countries and cultures.

Finally, how might the range of issues identified with postmodernity impact upon the exercise of pastoral care? This relates once again to the issue of personal identity, touched upon in the previous chapter, and an interpretation which suggests that identity is formed from within relationships rather than being a property of lone individuals pursuing their own objectives in ways determined by external traditions.

> Postmodern perspectives portray the self as a subject-in-relation, whose identity is forged within the complex interplay of economic, cultural and political factors. Contemporary pastoral/practical theology is gradually revising its own implicit ideals of the person to encompass such contexts. The subject of care is shifting from that of a self-actualized individual for whom care functions primarily at times of crisis towards one of a person in need of nurture and support as she or he negotiates a complexity of moral and theological challenges in a rapidly-changing economic and social context. (Graham 1996: 51)

Pastoral care involves equipping and resourcing people to cope with this context and the complexity created by and encountered in our working and domestic relationships. What this leads to is a growing diversity of pastoral practices and a broadening of those tasks beyond that of the ordained person. Graham herself argues that the Christian community is the appropriate locus for the exercise of pastoral care and that the objectives should go well beyond that of simply building up the faithful, and reach into the wider territory of economic and political life. I would agree with this but also suggest that the context with which we are currently engaged is more helpfully defined by the range of issues encountered in the study of globalization, which might well encompass the sort of challenges raised earlier by postmodernity. Yet it is also clear that Christian pastoral practice cannot engage effectively with, let alone critique, social and political life, unless it has its own vision of what it is to be human. It will be seen as the argument progresses that this question lies at the heart of practical theology's discussion with other disciplines.

The Range of Global Identities

We need to give close attention to the potential ways in which globalization is shaping the sense of human identity and for this I return initially to Rosenau. In addition to his range of 'Locals' he also suggests that there are a number of 'Globals' (Rosenau 2003: 119ff). He presents four types: Affirmative Globals, Resistant Globals, Specialized Globals and Territorial Globals. Once again it needs to be emphasized that these are 'ideal types' and must be handled with a degree of caution. They are useful to the extent that it enables us to recognize general trends in identity formation. Of particular interest are the ranks of Affirmative Globals, who appear to constitute a new elite.

> [They] consist mainly of persons whose organizational positions, intellectual achievements, artistic accomplishments, or other professional success cumulate and usually lead to extensive influence, wealth and respect ... that accord them access to the corridors of power ... These are the groups who are really in charge of time-space compression, who can really use it and turn it to advantage, whose power and influence it definitely increases. (Rosenau 2003: 122–3)

Included in this category are such people as top officials of the World Bank, the International Monetary Fund and the United Nations. These see themselves as players on a global stage and their energies and attentions are suitably directed. However, there are also other Affirmative Globals who are not in positions of such obvious influence, but are nevertheless comfortable and confident moving at this level, either for domestic or business purposes. They share with the others a readiness to move 'personally or electronically, widely around the ethnoscapes, mediascapes, financescapes, ideoscapes and technoscapes that constitute their world' (Rosenau 2003: 124).

The significance of this group for a traditional understanding of pastoral care and indeed for any importance of a sense of place is that they are less likely to be concerned about things that are happening in their immediate locality or what might be deemed to be their local community. Their world, or plausibility structure, is essentially global and this lifestyle might be described as 'high-tech nomadism'. They may well be in constant contact with others at great distance through their blackberries, mobile phones, e-mails and the other technical appendages of the global traveller. Being in contact is more important than being anywhere in particular.

Rosenau quotes some figures from a US airline, Star Alliance, a member of United Airlines, which has more than 32 million frequent fliers, with just under a million of these achieving elite status and more than 40,000 travelling on average 2,000 miles a week. One businessman, the chief executive of a worldwide advertising agency, flew over 360,000 miles on 128 flights during a 12-month period and this involved him being in the air for almost 34 days and took him to 40 cities in 24 countries. No doubt such figures could be repeated for a number of senior executives, although how this pattern of life is going to be sustainable given concerns over its environmental impact is a major question.

What is the impact of this type of existence upon one's sense of identity and belonging? There are no clear answers to this yet, but one might imagine that such mobility affects issues such as loyalty to one particular place and will certainly curtail the time and energy that people have to engage in any substantial activity at a local level. Identity confusion as one has to play a number of different roles in different cultures, but with increased frequency and rapidity, must be another possible consequence. The term 'Davos Man' has been coined in this context. Davos is the setting in Switzerland for the annual gathering of the World Economic Forum, the power-brokers, politicians and global celebrities who consider themselves to be the new elite.

In 1997 one thousand companies paid an annual membership of more than $13,000 which entitled them to attend the Davos meeting as well as smaller regional sessions throughout the year. To be a member a corporation has to have an annual volume of a billion Swiss francs and thus a global profile. A distinctive Davos culture is evident as a result, and one only has to access the website of the World Economic Forum to get a sense of who attends and where they stand within global power structures.

Although one must beware of assuming too great a degree of shared values and approaches one might argue that what binds Affirmative Globals together is that they are positive about the benefits of a globalizing world and not deterred by its potential for negative consequences.

> They may grant that the excesses of neoliberal economic policies need to be contained, and many probably perceive the need for greater transparency in the decisions and activities of corporations and NGOs, but rightly or wrongly, their optimism is so extensive that they tend not to see any need to engage in widespread public efforts to defend their ideas and interests. (Rosenau 2003: 136)

Rosenau's other categories of Globals are essentially variations on this central theme. Resistants are those who employ the technical advances of the global culture to resist its impact upon local identity and activity. Protestors against globalization at Seattle in 1999 would be an example, as might be religious groups concerned about the levels of global debt in the Jubilee 2000 movement. Terrorist groups organized along the lines of global networks but fighting to retain local autonomy and identity also seem possible candidates. Specialized and Territorial Globals are also more focused upon the global impact on specific local interests and positions and display a greater ambiguity towards the optimistic interpretation of the spread of a global economy and culture.

If all of this seems distant from the familiar pastoral setting of parish and congregation ministered to by a static professional within a distinct geographical locality, then that is exactly the point. Although there might still be the outward appearance of pastoral care exercised in this stable context, the reality is now more complex and confusing. What does it mean to exercise a pastoral ministry to those who are globally mobile and for whom 'there is no place like home', either because they no longer identify with a specific place or because they try extra hard to create such an identification because it contrasts with their everyday experience of life? There may be a polarization between giving no meaning at all to a locality and giving it an exaggerated meaning. The church is more likely to collude with the latter, but then may wonder why it becomes impossible to sustain local activity because nobody is actually around when you need them! Parishioners who have taken early retirement, and who are often the core of affluent parishes, invariably go away at weekends either to visit grandchildren or to take short holidays. Both place and locally based faith commitment become potential resources for identity construction but in new and unfamiliar ways in a global world. They are either of no significance, or of increased significance, rather than being the taken-for-granted background context of one's self-understanding.

The Self as Commodity

The human capacity to reduce oneself to an object is nothing new and one could argue that the commodification of the self has been a permanent feature of the human condition. However, it does seem that the forces of globalization have both intensified this process and shaped it in particular ways. Constructing oneself according to a specific brand or image is consistent with the commercial culture that operates on a global level, and the range of possibilities available, let alone the capability of changing one's image or persona as one moves rapidly from context to context, is a reflection of the mobility that is now a commonplace of global travel. The Christian tradition's view on this would be that it risks reducing human beings to products to be manipulated and exploited, and one would expect this to have an influence upon the exercise of a pastoral ministry.

The discourse of commodification is most familiar from political philosophy, and probably from its originally Marxist background, where labour is interpreted as having become a commodity within the capitalist economic system. It also affects the products that are central to this form of economic development, and therefore the means that are available to individuals to construct themselves, either by purchasing or owning those products which help to create a specific self-image, or in the public presentation of the self. One chooses who to become and purchases goods consistent with that image. This can also extend into relationships as one associates only with those others who match this profile.

As Giddens points out, this process can be seen as a reduction of the self to certain commercially based models and limits the possibilities of real self-development:

> To a greater or lesser extent, the project of the self becomes translated into one of the possession of desired goods and the pursuit of artificially framed styles of life. The consequences of this have often been noted. The consumption of ever-novel goods becomes in some part a substitute for the genuine development of self; appearance replaces essence as the visible signs of successful consumption come actually to outweigh the use-values of the goods and services in question themselves. (Giddens 1991: 198)

In case one might be tempted to think that this process applies only to the purchase of standard packages and products, one must be aware that it can also extend to the more outlandish and unorthodox aspects of contemporary culture. One can equally choose to construct oneself as an 'alternative' individual. Religious sources can be used as a resource from which to create such an individualized package.

The impact of mass markets, available because of the global economic system, and the influence of the media can be argued to have changed the scope and form of this type of self-construction. 'The mass media routinely present modes of life to which, it is implied, everyone should aspire; the lifestyles of the affluent are, in one form or another, made open to view and portrayed as worthy of emulation' (Giddens 1991: 199). Individuals want to identify with the celebrity culture that is presented to them on a daily basis. There is a danger that this process leads them into false assumptions about the predictability and controllability of normal life. One must, however, also recognize that humans are active agents and capable of viewing such images critically and thoughtfully, and therefore may reject the 'products' of the commercialized culture. Self-development requires the capacity to steer a course through the images and possibilities of self-construction presented with both a willingness to select between different packages, and also an awareness that the process itself needs to be understood as an outcome of an economic system that can be as damaging as it is exciting.

Practical theology has its own views on this and on the impact of globalization upon understandings of the self. The reduction of the person to a set of commercial products represents an essential loss of dignity and integrity. One's value as an individual becomes too closely identified with a specific set of purchases or position within a social system. Although this has always been a threat to human wholeness and well-being, globalization adds another dimension.

> The paradox of the global age is how human beings develop systems of commodification that create immense wealth, shape consciousness, and yet endanger the meaningfulness of life through unjust distribution or rampant consumerism. Understood from a Christian perspective, any and every attack on the worth of persons and God's good creation is to be resisted and transformed. (Schweiker 2000: 109)

The problems associated with this capacity to 'dispose of oneself' have been known for a long time and can be traced back as far as Troeltsch, according to Schweiker. The question is that of how much of myself I can 'sell off' before my integrity has been totally compromised. This can refer solely to labour power, but now equally applies to the current trend of creating oneself according to an externally determined image. It begs the question of what is of real value both within culture generally and more importantly within one's own life. Schweiker argues that the globalization of economic agents has accentuated the dangers of commercialization and commodification present within all cultures.

He suggests that any culture reproduces itself by informing the lives of its members with some set of beliefs about the world and specifically what is of value in human life. Within this it will also provide a hierarchy or ranking of attributes, so it may be that human relationships are seen as more important than possessions or ownership. Then there may well be a distinction between what is intrinsically valuable and those things that are of instrumental value because they contribute to other more significant 'goods'. The greatest power of a culture is to define and transmit those values and thus to shape the lives of its members. As Giddens says, global culture possesses this power in a way previously not encountered in human history, both through the impact of the media, and the fact that standardized packages are presented to people wherever they happen to live and work.

Its other great power is the spread of what is called an economic rationality which, as Schweiker suggests, is a cultural force that threatens to destroy the difference between intrinsic and instrumental goods:

> Not surprisingly, within a corporate economy it is increasingly difficult to give compelling reasons why something (say, persons or the common social good) ought to be respected and enhanced other than speaking of their use-value in maximizing economic utility. Insofar as 'money' is one of the languages, the currencies, of cultural reproduction in a market society, there is always the possibility that everything can be made and measured as a commodity. (Schweiker 2000: 124)

The question for religious traditions is the extent to which they appreciate how this process of self-construction is taking place and the ways in which their own resources have become raw material for this. There is an increased danger that such resources are reduced to instrumental value and thus fail to contribute towards a critique of a culture that is in danger of reducing human life to what is external and of fleeting value. Questions of justice and of the distribution of the goods of contemporary culture also figure in these discussions as global economics comes to determine the lives of people across the world irrespective of local traditions and cultures.

The Self as Consumer

Clearly linked to the process of commodification is the possibility that individuals now define themselves as consumers: 'I shop therefore I am'. Constructing oneself from the products of the surrounding culture depends upon the willingness and capacity to purchase the variety of consumer products now available in the global marketplace. As Gordon Lynch points out in his study of theology and popular culture, consumption is about so much more than simply meeting one's basic needs:

> In particular, consumption can be seen as an important way in which people express their personal and social identities, as well as their broader understanding of what it means to live a good and fulfilled life. (Lynch 2005: 60)

Identity and social status are expressed through the consumer products that one purchases, with certain of these being closely associated with a higher social standing and indeed with a 'snob value'. Lynch uses the work of the postmodern sociologist Baudrillard to argue that such products are of greater symbolic than of purely use value. The meaning of individual commodities can only be perceived once they are placed in the context of other commodities.

> The range of commodities available within a given society therefore each act as a kind of cultural language. The cultural 'meanings' associated with a Volvo car (e.g. safety, security, reliability) are, for example, different to those of a Porsche (conspicuous wealth) or a Citroen CV (conspicuous simplicity). By buying certain commodities … I am able to 'say' certain things about the kind of person I am and the kind of lifestyle that I wish to be associated with. (Lynch 2005: 62)

This is reflected in the current importance given to the goal of creating a brand or clearly identifiable product line that gives the 'right messages' to the people purchasing and to those who do not have the resources to make such a purchase. Even churches and congregations are likely to collude with this marketing approach as they attempt to draw in potential members, especially to the extent that they are aware of competing against other similar brands for their support. Lynch mentions the Alpha course as an example of this. Concentrating on a brand rather than a specific commodity gives the producer greater flexibility in the marketplace and the possibility of switching more easily to another product line, without losing a distinctive identity.

It is right, however, to guard against extreme interpretations of this process which risk excluding the human capacity for critique and for discrimination between brands or products. Most people know only too well that marketing techniques operate in this way and are therefore capable of making judgements accordingly. To conclude that individuals are prepared to accept being reduced to pure consumers would be a mistake. Religious traditions themselves build upon the importance of the symbolic value of everyday items and events, so are unlikely to simply separate themselves from this form of marketing. The important question is that of the extent to which individuals see themselves as autonomous agents who construct their sense of self through the processes of consumption, and the exercise of choice, in a supposedly open marketplace. Are both religion and the contemporary forms of spirituality to be encountered in a global context subject to this exercise of individual choice? To illuminate this issue further we turn to the work of a contemporary sociologist.

Zygmunt Bauman argues that current consumerism goes beyond the symbolic significance suggested by Baudrillard and has a more profound impact upon the construction of the self. Shopping is so much more than an activity in which we engage when we visit the obvious places of commercial exchange, as it has become the characteristic human response to all possibilities under the impact of the global economy. In a sense we now 'shop' for just about everything, including relationships and even religious or spiritual experiences. The reason for this is that shopping and consuming are not about the satisfaction of needs but rather the permanent non-satisfaction of desire. If we were ever to be satisfied by what we purchased or acquired then the shopping or consuming would cease and that would be self-defeating.

> It has been said that the spiritus movens of consumer activity is no longer the measurable set of articulated needs, but desire – a much more volatile and ephemeral, evasive and capricious, and essentially non-referential entity than 'needs', self-begotten and self-propelled motive that needs no other justification or 'cause'. Despite its successive and always short-lived reifications, desire has itself for its constant object, and for that reason is bound to remain insatiable however high the pile of other (physical or psychical) objects marking its past course may rise. (Bauman 2000: 75)

The objective of consumer culture is not to create products as such, but rather to create the constant consumer desire which fuels the process of consumption. This can only be sustained by a permanent culture of wish fulfilment, one that rushes people on from one image and ambition to another, so that what appeared to satisfy yesterday no longer satisfies today, and therefore has to be discarded and replaced by the latest fashion. Constant upgrading becomes the norm. This begins to undermine and challenge all notions of stability and continuity and therefore has an impact upon relationships and any sense of self or community. Simply offering a recognized brand or product (even within the field of religion) is no longer enough to capture the attention of potential constituents or consumers.

> Life organized around consumption … must do without norms: it is guided by seduction, ever rising desires and volatile wishes – no longer by normative regulation … The idea of 'luxury' makes little sense, as the point is to make today's luxuries into tomorrow's necessities, and to reduce the distance between 'today' and 'tomorrow' to the minimum – to 'take the waiting out of wanting'… The main concern is therefore that of adequacy – of being 'ever ready', of having the ability to rise to the opportunity when it comes, to develop new desires made to the measure of new, previously unheard-of and unexpected allurements. (Bauman 2000: 76–7)

The problem is that nothing lasts and that everything is 'for the time being only'. Whatever has been presented as the norm and now dominates people's thoughts and ambitions is destined to become defunct within the near future. There seems to be something inherently perverse and apparently corrosive of stable relationships and structures in this and thus it is opposed to the basis on which most religious life is normally organized. Life becomes reduced to 'one-offs' or 'spectaculars' which are repeated at one's peril because the second-time around they have already gone stale and represent a failure of effort and imagination. One can see this now in the tendency to produce single worship events which are designed not to be reproduced.

If Bauman is right on this – and one can certainly recognize these tendencies in contemporary life, which drive people to continue constructing and reconstructing their self-image on a regular basis – then it has implications for practical theology and requires a basis for critique, if it is not to become a destructive force in pastoral relationships. On the other hand, it might be that the elusive and fleeting points of pastoral contact may now have to form one of the more common bases for encounter, and that congregational life formerly based upon stability and continuity has to shed yet another zombie category in order to adapt. Before making a definitive judgement we need to look at further impacts of globalization upon the construction of the self.

The Self as Project

One of the most significant contributions to this debate has been the work of the sociologist Castells (2001). His argument is that the impact of globalization creates an environment within which there are three basic options available to individuals in this process of identity construction. These are legitimizing identity, resistance identity and project identity. As it is possible to recognize each one of these in the contemporary sphere of pastoral care it is necessary to devote space to their description.

Castells makes it clear that identity is to be distinguished from the understanding of role. Roles might be, for instance, being a worker, a mother, a union member, a church-goer or a footballer. While these might become a part of a person's identity, if they are important enough, they are not to be equated with identity construction. Identities are sources of meaning for the individuals themselves and therefore have to be internalized. So identity is an organization of meaning while role is more to do with function. Castells believes that in what he calls 'the network society', which is his way of describing the social effects of globalization, such meaning is based upon a primary identity, one that becomes the framework for the other multiple identities that make up our lives.

The focus here is on collective rather than individual identity and the importance of this for pastoral care will become clear as the argument progresses. Here are Castells' definitions of the three types of identity.

- Legitimizing identity is 'introduced by the dominant institutions of society to extend and rationalize their domination vis à vis social actors'
- Resistance identity is 'generated by those actors that are in positions/conditions devalued and/or stigmatized by the logic of domination, thus building trenches of resistance and survival on the basis of principles different from, or opposed to, those permeating the institutions of society'
- Project identity is 'when social actors, on the basis of whichever cultural materials are available to them, build a new identity that redefines their position in society and, by so doing, seek the transformation of overall social structure' (Castells 2001: 8).

The question for practical theology is where most parishioners might fit within this schema and how religious resources might be used to construct whichever of these identities become primary. There are obvious points of contact with Rosenau's work on different types of Locals and Globals, but the concentration here is clearly on the collective rather than the individual.

Castells uses this categorization to show how each of these leads to a specific social form. Legitimizing identity generates civil society, those organizations and institutions within society that tend to reinforce existing power structures, and he names as examples of this, churches, trade unions, political parties and other civic associations. These are the structures that stand between the individual and the state but which often become sites of conflict when one or the other seeks to extend its influence. It needs to be recognized that Castells is employing a particular interpretation of civil society that others might contest, seeing it as an emancipatory force in political life. He is arguing that these institutions and social groupings tend to support and legitimize existing configurations of power. Hence churches, for instance, might be seen as reinforcing the status quo, and as therefore a form of social control and of keeping people 'in their place'.

Resistance identity leads instead to the formation of communes or communities, in the sense of tightly bounded and distinct groupings that see themselves over against the rest of the world. This might be based on a feeling of alienation or discrimination and form around an ethnic, national and religious identity.

> Religious fundamentalism, territorial communities, nationalist self-affirmation, or even the pride of self-denigration, inverting the terms of oppressive discourse (as in the 'queer culture' of some tendencies in the gay movement), are all expressions of what I name 'the exclusion of the excluders by the excluded'. That is, the building of defensive identity in the terms of dominant institutions/ideologies, reversing the value judgement while reinforcing the boundary. (Castells 2001: 9)

It is important to note that this was written before 9/11 and the subsequent heightened debate around the role of religious fundamentalism or 'furious religion'. Yet it is clear that the role of religion in forming the grounds for a resistance to global forces is evident even before this date and that religious beliefs and practices are potential sources for constructing a particular response to a perceived threat to a deeply held identity and culture.

Project identity is the most difficult to define, but refers to the capacity of human subjects to envision different and alternative futures. I will argue in due course that this is the most important aspect of identity construction to be considered by practical theology and must have links with other social movements that are now familiar, such as feminism and environmentalism, but also that Christianity has a specific contribution to offer. However, I now want to redescribe these categories in terms that I suggest are instructive for understanding the impact of globalization on practical theology.

The role of religion within society can be either legitimating, integrating or critical. Legitimation is close to Castells' first category in that one can see how religious beliefs and practices are frequently employed – not necessarily consciously or deliberately – to support and sustain existing social and political structures. Those familiar with interpretations of rural ministry, for instance, will recognize the idea that the Church of England in such areas depended upon collusion between the squire and the parson in maintaining a hierarchical social order. Although this might have appeared to have been destroyed as villages are taken over by incomers and commuters, there are still strong elements of this to be found. Every locality still has its 'establishment' and religious groups need to locate themselves somewhere within the local hierarchies however they might be formed. Those social structures reproduce themselves by repeating existing patterns of 'acceptable' behaviour.

Perhaps the most familiar social impact of religious groups though is the integrating function. For many people being part of a local church or congregation offers a sense of belonging and integrating into a community, and this may well be the most important attraction of joining up. This operates for those who have suffered a recent trauma such as bereavement, but also for those who move into a locality and are searching for a way of becoming part of and integrating into the local community. Particularly in locations where the local church perceives itself to be 'at the heart of community life' or even a significant feature of that, drawing people in on the basis that they will find a role within the locality is a well-established method of recruiting new members. Most congregations have other activities associated with the regular worshipping community, for instance, fund-raising or social events, choirs, young people's work of some description, and the task is to find which aspect of this individuals or families might fit into.

As one examines more closely how this specific strategy contributes to the exercise of pastoral care, it becomes evident that this form of belonging, and therefore the nature of the integrating identity, is another zombie category, or, at least, not quite what it used to be given the different identities that are forming in response to globalization. What belonging now means to many people is a subject that requires detailed research, but we have already seen in earlier chapters that it is likely to be more tenuously related to a sense of place and a shared history. Greater social mobility and a tendency to 'consume' community are becoming familiar characteristics of collective social activity. What is meant by this is that people will choose to join and belong to particular groups for a limited period only and for as long as it appears to serve their own specific interests. As Bauman suggests, the pattern now is likely to be that of 'for the time being only', until something better or more appropriate comes along.

This social behaviour is particularly noticeable in church-based children's and young people's work and also in matters of the selection of schooling. Parental choice appears to be the prime directive, partly because of more traditional social barriers, but now also under the auspices of a global culture within which competition for employment and social opportunities is perceived to be the greatest threat to future stability. I must secure the very best for my child, and that means from the earliest age through nursery and playgroup right through to senior school and university, if they are to stand a chance of surviving in a world where the established economic base of manufacturing has slipped away to developing countries such as China and India and the future requires adaptability and the widest possible range of skills and social contacts. Global forces directly impact upon parental choice and therefore their willingness, or otherwise, to engage in local activity.

Integrating communities therefore are now of a subtly different nature. They are much more likely to be 'communities of interest' than communities of commitment to a specific institution or activity that is valued for its own sake. The nature of or the motivation behind commitment has changed under the impact of global influences. Hence many local groups are finding it both more difficult to recruit leaders and to retain members. This is a complex phenomenon that cannot just be attributed to changes in community life, but it is certain that this is one of the major features of church life in recent years. Governance requirements and the drive towards professionalization which are themselves possible responses to globalization are other significant influences upon the difficulties now faced by local groups.

From the point of view of pastoral care there is one immediate consequence of these changes. The nature of the relationships formed within locally based church groups is becoming more instrumental and based upon personal ties and commitment. What matters is what belonging to this specific group can do for me (or for my family), and how long I want to sustain the personal friendships with the other people involved. I have coined the term 'enclaves of interim intimacy' as a way of describing this change in integrating communities. There is a danger that such groups become socially monochrome and relatively enclosed, rather than being 'open to the other' in ways that Christian groups perhaps should be. They are 'interim' in the sense that, as Bauman argues, they will be 'for the time being only'. They will also depend more heavily upon the quality and particular personal relationships and friendships, rather than upon a commitment to the activity or institution, and are therefore more likely to fracture when those go wrong (Reader 2005: 65). The relationships and the belonging are a means to an end rather than an end in themselves, once the current culture of choice becomes the dominant perspective.

If this is what is happening, then it changes the whole ethos and nature of the sort of community life which is itself a strategy for encountering others, and thus also a location for the exercise of pastoral care. Constructing integrating community as a key aspect of local church life has a different meaning for many of the people participating from that which it might have for the minister and older members of a congregation. This may only emerge when people who have been recruited withdraw their interest or energy and transfer their allegiances elsewhere, which is to be expected if these are in fact communities of interest and enclaves of interim intimacy. Frustration and a sense of failure that it was not possible to sustain commitment, and even the activity itself, then take over.

A question for ministers and congregations is that of whether to engage in this type of activity at all if it is now clear that the 'communities' that form as a result are significantly different from those that are the supposed object of the exercise. Does it matter that those who participate in church-based activities do so for the time being only and with different expectations and a different understanding of the commitment? This constitutes another blurred boundary and suggests that the tried and tested model of community life associated with local churches is yet another zombie category..

I will argue that the only way to resolve this issue is by an appeal to a vision of the project identity or what I prefer to call the critical function of Christian social engagement.

The Political Dimension of Pastoral Care

It will be recalled from the initial discussion based on Graham's analysis of the changing context of pastoral care that one of the major challenges facing the subject is to respond to the social and political determinants of people's lives. Rather than embarking upon the full scale debate about alternative visions of what it is to be human, I will refer to a specific example which illustrates how this aspect links to the topic of globalization. I assume that one can argue that it is better to offer a critique of the present by suggesting alternatives which point out ways in which things could be improved. The Christian tradition must have a contribution to make here if it is to engage with the most significant contemporary political issues.

Previous sections have concentrated on how it might be possible to offer pastoral care within the changed context of relatively affluent and secure societies. However, a weakness of this approach is that it ignores the plight of those across the world who might be seen as the victims of globalization. A political approach to pastoral care would surely want to address this and to raise questions about the policies and decisions that support the power structures which hold people within the enclosures of poverty, war and economic insecurity. Where are the possible thresholds to a better life for those who are 'at the sharp end' of globalization, and how might religious beliefs and values contribute to establishing the basis for a critique of global injustice?

It is important to register that this debate is now re-establishing itself at the heart of the political philosophy agenda and in a way that has not been true since before the fall of the Berlin Wall in 1989. One of the key dynamics which has determined political philosophy in the last decade is that there is supposedly no longer a viable alternative to Western global capitalism and a particular version of democracy that is seen to go with it. It is only in the last few years that this discussion has reopened through a combination of different approaches, and it will be crucial for religious ideas to engage with this if they are to get recognition for their alternative vision.

Graham, writing in 1996, expressed the view that postmodernity was then the emerging conversation partner for pastoral theology and providing the central ideas to which the subject needed to respond. Things have moved on since then in that globalization is now taking centre stage in these debates. The question now is whether there is any alternative to liberal capitalism. Hence these comments from a political philosopher who stands broadly within the Marxist tradition:

> The 1990s were marked by a significant shift in the intellectual and political environment. The very scale of the triumph of liberal capitalism after the end of the Cold War and the attempts via international financial institutions such as the IMF and the World Bank to universalize the neo-liberal economic package known as the Washington Consensus made how – and whether – to live with capitalism an increasingly urgent issue. (Callinicos 2006: 51)

The 'battle at Seattle' can be seen as part of this movement of protest as indeed can the Jubilee 2000 process which challenged world leaders to address the problems of Third World debt. Callinicos argues that the tide began to turn intellectually with the publication of two texts, the first by the French sociologist Bourdieu, who had previously kept his distance from direct political involvement (Bourdieu 1993), and the second by the French philosopher Derrida entitled *Spectres of Marx* (1993). The first text brought together a series of accounts from across the world to illustrate how ordinary people's lives were being adversely affected by liberal capitalism, and, in the second:

> Derrida denounced the evils constitutive of the 'new world order' – unemployment, exclusion, competition, debt, the arms trade, nuclear proliferation, war, globalized crime, the domination of international institutions by the Great Powers and the big corporations. (Callinicos 2006: 52)

The problem that Callinicos seeks to address and to which the discussion will return, is that of establishing the basis for a critique of liberal capitalism which is not simply a return to Marxism and that therefore no longer carries credibility. In a sense the question for practical theology is similar: how to establish a basis for critique from within a Christianity that has too many zombie categories and no longer carries any substantial public credibility.

However, it is important to recognize that these emerging questions arise not only from within a post-Marxist frame of reference but also more generally within political philosophy. Thus Will Hutton, standing within the social democratic model, also refers to the issues of equality and injustice that face current global economic and political configurations. Referring to the work of the economist Amartya Sen, who has been an influential figure in development economics, and also to the philosopher John Rawls, Hutton argues that inequality has to be seen as morally, socially, economically and humanly offensive.

> The foundation of human association is the idea that human life has equal worth and human beings are equally entitled to political, economic and social rights which will allow them to choose a life they have reason to value. But without powerful countervailing forces, the accident of birth will always predict the rights to which one effectively has access, and thus one's capacity to choose a life one values. (Hutton 2007: 204)

So Rawls and Sen agree on the need for a social safety net to ensure a basic standard of living, basic human rights, equality of opportunity and accountability of political decision-makers. Although the details of this sort of programme will be in dispute and the actual content of such rights and their extent will also be a matter of controversy, Hutton is clear that this general framework is now emerging as at least the basis for a critique of the current ills of liberal capitalism. Somewhere within this debate religious beliefs need to find their voice if they are to establish an effective political dimension to their pastoral concerns in response to the forces of globalization.

One such example of this in action is a recent report presented to the General Synod of the Church of England on the subject of asylum seekers and refugees (Skinner 2005). It can certainly be argued that globalization has contributed to the growing numbers in both categories and that Western nations face the challenge of their response to this problem. Contrary to public opinion in the UK for instance, which sees the country as a 'soft touch' for asylum seekers, the evidence paints a very different picture. It is actually the countries which are the direct neighbours of states that are experiencing conflict, civil war and persecution who are taking most refugees and asylum seekers. Of the 14.5 million refugees in the world, 5 million are in Asia and 1 million are in Peshawar in Pakistan.

During 1992–2001, an estimated 86 per cent of the world's refugees originated from developing countries, which also provided asylum to 72 per cent of them. In proportion to the countries' size, population and wealth, the countries taking the greatest burden are Iran, Burundi and Guinea.

Although the details of this may seem beyond the scope of this book, what is most significant about the report is its attempt to establish a theological basis for a critique of current UK government practice and the distortions of popular public opinion as shaped by the media.

Skinner draws upon the work of Derrida and his notion of unconditional hospitality as a means of showing that the Christian response to those who are in need and at the sharp end of global politics demands much more than Western governments are prepared to offer. This is important both because it displays an alternative view of what it is to be human and also because it suggests that resources from other traditions can fruitfully be brought into dialogue with Christian ideas. As Skinner says:

> The unconditional welcoming of Others acknowledges both the best and worst possibilities of the interaction. The relationship of trust between strangers is an example of the 'social capital' that many churches demonstrate in their work with refugees and asylum seekers. Derrida's thinking on hospitality strove to distinguish between inclusion and assimilation. This reflects another important aspect of hospitality towards asylum seekers and refugees. Whilst accepting and welcoming them into one's own space, the aim is not to acculturate or assimilate individuals so they simply reflect oneself. Each person's individuality must be affirmed as reflecting the diversity of God's creation, and the sanctity of each life upheld. (Skinner 2005: 12)

So here is a working example of ways in which pastoral care can be shaped and supported from within the Christian tradition in response to the victims of globalization. It addresses the collective and political dimension of the problem by establishing an alternative vision of human becoming drawing on both Christian and external sources. However, this is just the beginning of a more wide-ranging debate that will be developed in later chapters. Pastoral care is changing rapidly and one major reason for this is the impact of globalization.

Chapter 4

Worship, Spirituality and Globalization

Introduction

In the previous chapter it became clear that it is necessary to have some grounds for a critique of current culture and practice in order to suggest alternatives to the more questionable consequences of globalization. Pastoral care presupposes an understanding of what it is to be human and the specific suggestion was presented that a version of Derrida's notion of hospitality might form the basis of this. This however is only the beginning of a more detailed and complex discussion to which this chapter is a further contribution. It was argued that various reductionist views of human nature, for instance, the self as consumer or commodity, need to be challenged from within the Christian tradition as they fail to do justice to a complete picture of what humans are destined to be or to become according to the understanding of this tradition. Yet it is likely that exactly such views are encountered amongst those who have become willing subjects of global processes. The logical extension of this problem is an examination of what is happening within the areas of worship and spirituality, themselves closely connected to the study of pastoral care and a central concern for practical theology.

This also provides an opportunity to return to the themes identified at the beginning of the book and that offer a framework for the Christian engagement with globalization. Thus one might ask whether there is a blurring of boundaries occurring, where the enclosures are and the thresholds might be emerging, and how a concept of reflexivity might illuminate the discussion. The subsequent examination of both worship and spirituality will reveal that each of these can indeed be helpful in interpreting current trends within both areas. The starting point though is a specific argument about the impact of globalization upon a particular aspect of worship, that of the Eucharist, not perhaps the most obvious area for examination, but in fact one that will highlight some of the more theoretical elements that require attention.

Globalization and the Eucharist

This is a critical exposition of a book that stands within the movement known as Radical Orthodoxy, a theological approach associated with the work of John Milbank (1990) but which has spawned a series of related publications from other authors. Although some of this work is deeply philosophical and not necessarily the most accessible for practical theology, it has the merit of penetrating to the theoretical issues from a theological perspective and at least offering a critique of current responses and practice (Cavanaugh 2002).

Cavanaugh begins his argument by stating that Christian social thought is in a state of confusion regarding the phenomenon of globalization. It is tempted to continue as if nothing significant has changed and that church-based engagement with the public realm can safely assume that this needs to take place within an imaginary national space because this is still where conflicts are settled. The study of globalization is left to those who bemoan the impact of global economics upon the obvious victims of these forces in the developing world. The other possibility is that Christians welcome a world in which borders are increasingly being transgressed because this somehow presages precisely the unity or catholicity which is the church's vision for the future. But has the world of global capital now superseded that hope for a re-united humanity?

As an alternative, Cavanaugh presents an understanding of the Eucharist, thus proposing that this central aspect of worship itself stands as a critique of globalization:

> I believe that much of the Christian confusion over globalization results from a neglect of the Eucharist as the source of a truly Catholic practice of space and time; I would like to juxtapose this geography with another geography, a geography of the Eucharist and its production of catholicity. (Cavanaugh 2002: 98)

His argument is that globalization is not properly characterized by mere fragmentation, but enacts a universal mapping of space typified by a detachment from any particular localities. But what this achieves is a discipline which reproduces the divisions between the rich and the poor and the creation of fragmented subjects who are unable to engage with a catholic imagination of space and time. So globalization is a master narrative, one which claims universal truth and authority for itself, but also one which produces fragmented subjects who are incapable of telling a genuinely catholic story. The only counterpoint to this will be the Eucharist itself, which is focused on the body of Christ and which collapses all spatial and temporal divisions.

It is important to recognize some of the familiar elements of the debate: first the issue of the relationship between global and local which has featured heavily in the first three chapters and the question of where Christianity stands on this, both in practice and in theory. It appears that Cavanaugh is falling into the camp of those who identify globalization with fragmentation and localization with integration, a view which Rosenau challenges as an inaccurate description of the social and political processes. Is there more of a blurring of boundaries than Cavanaugh is inclined to accept?

His categorization of globalization as a master narrative has echoes of the arguments of such thinkers as Hardt and Negri (and Cavanaugh himself refers to the work of Hardt) when they suggest that Empire is a new enclosure which so dominates the world that it is difficult to see if there is any 'outside' or thresholds to other possibilities. This is one of the crucial issues for consideration as he suggests. Is there any scope for human freedom or autonomy, or have the forces of globalization become so all-consuming that it is impossible to see beyond them let alone form a viable alternative to global capitalism? Whether Cavanaugh's interpretation of the Eucharist can create this alternative is a matter for further debate.

Finally, Cavanaugh's focus on what type of subjects are being created by globalization links directly with the discussion about which vision of human being is at work here and how this might be challenged and critiqued from within the Christian tradition. His suggestion is that we are dealing with the sort of fragmented subjects determined by the desires underlying consumption and who also turn themselves into commodities in order to market themselves in the competitive global economy. So there is considerable support for exactly the concerns expressed in our discussion of pastoral care.

The Dominance of the Universal

Cavanaugh's starting point is that globalization does not in fact herald the demise of the nation state – an argument that is now well-established within political sociology – but that it is in fact a hyperextension of the nation state's project of subsuming the local under the universal. It is a further stage in the process by which the state has usurped the former powers of the church, the nobility, guilds, clans and towns. This refers to a previous discussion in which Cavanaugh challenges the conventional view that the creation of the liberal-democratic nation state was a reaction against the 'wars of religion' and thus a deliberate attempt to extract faith from the public world of politics and commerce (Cavanaugh 2002: 26). He argues that the economic and political movements to oust the influence of religion had already begun. Whether or not one agrees with this, it highlights the centrality of the relationship between religion and politics which is a continuing concern for practical theology.

Milbank's suggestion that the 'simple space' between the sovereign and the individual of this previous era is replaced by a complex space of overlapping loyalties and authorities is uncritically adopted by Cavanaugh. The issue that arises for Christians is how they are to relate to the public world, which is clearly a central question for this book.

The classic interpretation of the next stage of development is that the continued rise of the state creates an intermediate space, now often termed civil society, within which one finds institutions such as churches, trade unions, voluntary organizations and even families. Some political theorists have held that civil society is the most promising location for the opposition and critique of state power and have placed faith groups firmly within this territory, but this is now in question as the powers of the state appear to increase and encroach more deeply into this area of supposed independence. So is the area of civil society an enclosure or a threshold, and under what conditions, as the boundaries between the two become increasingly blurred under globalization? If civil society no longer offers a serious alternative to the global economy is another possibility to be found?

Cavanaugh suggests that the process of globalization has now gone so far that civil society can no longer present an effective challenge to global forces. The local is now so firmly subsumed beneath the universal because it has become detached from any particular space. He uses now familiar descriptions in order to support this view:

> Governments have ceded or lost control over the transnational economy; through deregulation and computer transfers, money has become virtually stateless. The disciplinary mechanisms of the factory and the factory town are no longer necessary for the extraction of surplus labour, and have given way to part-time labour, home labour, various forms of illegal labour, and global 'outsourcing' … Unions have consequently lost much of their power. With the loss of geographical stability, family, Church and local community have also given way to global monoculture and 'virtual community'. (Cavanaugh 2002: 103)

Once again there is considerable common ground with the discussion in the previous chapters about the changing nature of community relationships and attachment to a sense of place and ways in which these have become zombie categories within this new configuration.

What is most significant for Cavanaugh's argument is that this version of the universal created by globalization has now come to dominate the local and particular in such a way that it is damaging not only to individuals but also to international relationships. Even apparent attachments to the local are now subject to the determining forces of globalization as areas attempt to establish their 'unique selling points' and a clear basis for their marketability. This heightens competition between different 'locals' and risks destabilizing relationships between potential trading partners, for instance. Diversity and difference are an illusion, as they are simply the images that are required to be distinct in the global economy. One of my criticisms of Radical Orthodoxy is that it has fallen prey to exactly this tendency to present a clear and distinct 'product' in order to compete in the global market place of religions (Reader 1997: 144).

One can see how important this debate is for discussion of the changing role of worship and spirituality in the context of globalization. At what point does Christianity begin to present itself as a distinct and clearly identifiable product in order to improve its recruitment now it is placed alongside other forms of faith and spirituality which are immediately accessible in bookshops and on the internet? Where does one draw the line between worship and entertainment given the pressure to compete against all the other attractions that are now on offer on Sundays? How can the local and the particular retain any degree of integrity and authenticity in a world where fleeting appearances are the basis for attention and everything is 'for the time being only', as Bauman suggests?

Cavanaugh himself pursues this argument to its logical conclusion and suggests that all aspects of the local become images, and therefore commodities to be marketed, thus able to transcend boundaries in ways necessary for survival in the global marketplace. But of course this also has an impact upon the self, as identity is increasingly constructed from this welter of conflicting and disparate images which are presented to us as desirable and essential for the illusion of success. All products are disposable and ephemeral, simply the latest component for self creation until something more attractive and fashionable comes along.

How then is Christian worship and spirituality to retain its identity and integrity, let alone form the basis for a critique of this globalized culture? What is to say that it is not becoming simply another resource which may or may not appeal to people as a useful element for one's latest version of oneself? Cavanaugh's answer is the

Eucharist, and he claims that it offers a counter-narrative of global proportions. This is so because the true catholicity produced by the Eucharist does not depend on the mapping of global space which underpins the global economy. It overcomes the dichotomy of the universal and the local, collapsing the spatial divisions not by mobility but by gathering in the local assembly.

> The Eucharist is a decentred centre; it is celebrated in the multitude of local churches scattered throughout the world, with a great diversity of rites, music and liturgical spaces. It is precisely this fact that complexifies the calculus of particular and universal within the Church catholic. (Cavanaugh 2002: 114)

A danger with this, as Cavanaugh himself is aware, is that it becomes simply a retreat into a place-bound theocracy or sect, so the local is privileged as a site of resistance to global forces by virtue of being a place. But he argues that this will not do, as the Eucharist is not a place as such, but rather a story which performs certain spatial operations on places. The individual is engaged in a process of movement or journey and it is the itinerary, not the places themselves, which is most important. The particular is always drawn into this but only as a staging post on the way to the Heavenly City and not because it has a significance of its own on some global map.

> But this pilgrimage is not the detachment from any and all spaces, the sheer mobility of globalism. The Eucharist journeys by telling a story of cosmic proportions within the particular face-to-face encounter of neighbours and strangers in the local Eucharistic gathering. In an economy of hypermobility, we resist not by fleeing, but by abiding. (Cavanaugh 2002: 117)

I will next raise some questions and reservations about his solution to the problem of how Christianity might be a site of resistance to the excesses of global capitalism. The value of his book is that it draws out issues which are central for practical theology as it engages with globalization and one can agree with his analysis without agreeing with the proposed antidote.

Even though Cavanaugh claims that he is not creating an alternative place as such, what he is clearly doing is creating an alternative structure or institution which must maintain a critical distance from globalization in order to offer a viable alternative or threshold. So the church becomes the privileged locus for resistance because without this institution there would be no continued practice or authorization of the Eucharist. One might note that the classic Marxist approach was to claim that the proletariat was the privileged locus of resistance to capitalism – the working class was going to become the herald and forerunner of the revolution. Perhaps such claims are inescapable, but one does need to question this process and wonder why and how it is always one's own particular group who become the 'chosen ones'. There is a further question of whether such groups and institutions are capable of offering appropriate resistance or whether it is now networks and/or individuals who stand more of a chance of creating convincing alternatives.

Another problem with Radical Orthodoxy is its idealization both of the past and also of the church itself in its current configuration. Was the world ever quite as dominated by the religious powers as both Milbank and Cavanaugh suggest, or is this in itself an interpretation of history presented by the religious authorities to justify their later claims to power? In what ways does the church now resemble the picture presented by such authors and, if, as seems obvious, the reality is one of division and dissension over a whole range of issues, what does it mean to say that Christians are united through their participation in the Eucharist? What is the exact relationship between the local and the global within Christianity and what practical purchase do such theories have upon the reality of church life? One needs to approach Cavanaugh's solution to the challenge of globalization with a degree of scepticism, but he helpfully points towards the development of the discussion, notably in the area of what it means to be human. If his is not the answer then an alternative needs to be constructed.

Worship Disembedded

While there is clearly value in reviewing both the theory and ideals of Christian worship as expressed by Cavanaugh, it is probably the practicalities that dominate the thoughts of those engaged in practical theology. Have global influences significantly changed the context in which worship takes place and what might be the impact of this? I have entitled this section 'Worship Disembedded' because I think one can argue that this is one of the central features of a globalized culture and that it brings into question both the traditional form and content of this element of Christian practice.

Anglican worship presupposes stable and settled congregations and a regular pattern of services guaranteeing familiarity and a security of structure. If one doubts this, then one need only recall the controversy surrounding the introduction of the *Alternative Service Book* (ASB) in 1980. The introduction of the revised services caused consternation amongst church-goers not simply because of the use of more modern language, but because it provided greater choice and required people to think about and select from a menu of possibilities rather than following the prescribed orders. This process had begun with earlier revisions, but the ASB was seen as the logical culmination of these. One of the major objections was that the whole idea of common prayer, whereby one could worship anywhere in the country and know what one was going to encounter, was now compromised by this reformulation. Thus the further revision known as Common Worship 20 years later made a conscious attempt to return to a degree of common structure and greater consistency of practice.

This debate continues, and whether or not an appropriate balance has been struck it is perhaps too early to tell. There are both generational and cultural issues within the Church of England and also continuing arguments about whether greater areas of flexibility and freedom are now required by younger people who have grown up without any experience of the Book of Common Prayer and Anglican worship as it used to be. In support of the revisions it was argued that the culture had already changed and that worship was starting to reflect this through an increasingly diverse practice carried out despite the familiar and tested structures. Both the ASB and subsequently Common Worship were simply recognitions of this and attempts to give this growing diversity proper form and authority.

This is certainly relevant to discussions about the impact of globalization as it reflects the tendency of individuals to construct their own personal versions of religious traditions even when coming together to share these with others through worship. Yet there is a deeper question of the extent to which what appear to be familiar and acceptable patterns of worship are now becoming zombie categories. Although the outward forms are the same; is the inner experience and meaning structure attached to worship now different as a result of wider cultural changes? If people's lives are increasingly disembedded and no longer attached to either locality or to a stable set of relationships dependent upon dwelling in one place over time, then will this not also have an effect upon what worship means to those involved? Perhaps the shape now taken by weddings, where the church chosen is more likely to be determined by childhood associations or even aesthetic considerations than by residence, is a clue to how things are different. The fact that there are now an increasing number of gathered congregations who choose which acts of worship to attend, and will travel to do so, rather than feeling restricted to their local church, is another aspect of these changes. Instead of being 'committed' to a specific place or building because that is where one has lived for years or happens to reside now, one selects the service that 'suits', much as one selects other consumer goods that are desirable at the time.

It is because of these growing tendencies for people to 'shop around' that ministers feel themselves under pressure to provide a 'worship product' that will attract potential recruits. Worship thus becomes subject to the consumer and commodity mentality that is the exact opposite of what theologians such as Cavanaugh present as their counter-cultural interpretation of the Eucharist. Has worship now gone too far in the direction of offering what could be a form of spiritual entertainment and thus compromised its integrity in the process? Is there an alternative if the former pattern of worship belonging to a stable congregation with secure and familiar relationships over time is becoming a thing of the past and limited to ageing attenders and dwindling numbers? Where might one draw the line in this blurring of boundaries, and what is the possibility that the experience of worship might yet be a threshold into other possibilities rather than being a reflection of a consumerist culture?

The Media and Worship

The challenge of this debate is to steer a middle course between forms of theological idealism, as encountered in Cavanaugh, for instance, and, at the other extreme, a version of technological or cultural determinism which would suggest that worship is now wholly under the influence of external forces. A particular version of the latter is to argue that people's tastes and habits are now so shaped by the media that all forms of worship are inevitably forced to adopt their characteristics and to become subject to the commercial forces that influence them. Discussions about the role of TV are to the fore in this discussion.

There are those who have argued that the form in which material now appears, itself determines the content of what is being communicated. If this is so then it must have implications for how people are now accustomed to receive information or to experience public events. So, for instance, oral cultures will tend to encourage stories and proverbs that maintain the wisdom of traditions and cultures in ways that can be easily communicated and remembered through spoken communication. Narrative will be a characteristic aspect of such cultures. Other cultures will depend more heavily upon the written word and produce texts that pass on their wisdom and ideas. Christian tradition clearly stands within this cultural context and the interpretation of texts has been central to its reproduction over time, so Scriptures, moral codes, doctrines and creeds are to be found within its patterns of worship.

The growing impact of the electronic media, particularly TV and its various offshoots, could well have changed the forms in which people are able to respond to ideas. Gordon Lynch of Birmingham University presents the argument that TV has now reduced all information to entertainment (Lynch 2005: 79). This, if true, affects not only religion but also politics and all other forms of public presentation, and severely limits the capacity for rational open debate about serious issues. There is a further implication of this also:

> In a culture dominated by television, the details of a politician's ideas become less important than their media image or their ability to communicate effectively through media-friendly 'sound-bites'. Similarly in the context of religion, there can be an increasing pressure to lead religious services in entertaining ways (evident for example in the 'Seeker Services' model developed in the Willow Creek Church). (Lynch 2005: 79–80)

Anybody who has been involved in a BBC Songs of Praise programme, for instance, will understand the pressure to select items that are short, visually effective and immediately accessible to a television audience. The idea that one could use TV to communicate a series of ideas and arguments, as might be done through a written text, for a popular show – even though this particular one appeals to a traditional and probably elderly Christian clientele – is simply laughable. The pattern of a mixture of well-known hymns juxtaposed with swift interviews relating to personal and emotional events has now become familiar for special services organized by churches as a result of the success of such TV programmes. What works on the small screen is increasingly adopted in acts of worship and then shapes the content of what is being communicated. Novelty and the introduction of spectacular 'one-off' events, to stave off the inevitable routine and boredom that are more characteristic of regular worship, find their way into the life of the churches because this is what people are accustomed to be offered and to which they are inclined to respond.

As Lynch suggests though, one must beware of sinking into a form of technological determinism which underestimates the human capacity to be critical of what is presented. We all know – on one level at least – how the media operate, and how they both try to shape our experience as well as being shaped by our cultural requirement for immediate access and entertainment. Other experiences are still available and television does not determine our consciousness in quite such an all-embracing fashion. One might also argue that part of the challenge for worship leaders in this changed environment is to find ways of using the new media to communicate the Christian message in a non-reductionist form. Using different methods of communication does not necessarily compromise the integrity of the message, although one needs to be aware of their limitations and dangers – but then, the same must also be said of oral communication and the written word. The classic Anglican response is to provide a 'mixed menu' of services which appeal to a variety of constituencies with the hope that people will be willing to experience forms with which they are less familiar, to see if they can appreciate other expressions of religious commitment and spirituality. However, beneath this plurality of approaches there is still the question of what understanding of human being is being communicated, and whether or not this might be consistent with a Christian vision.

Current Interest in Spirituality

One of the arguments emerging from the field of religious studies is that there is a revived and growing interest in spirituality (Heelas and Woodhead 2005; Partridge 2004). Quite what explanations are available and how significant this is are matters to be examined shortly, but first I present some empirical evidence to support this claim. At this point I will not attempt to enter the vexed subject of definitions of the term. Whatever people mean by spirituality, there is an argument that current levels of interest are on the increase and that this is at least partly due to global influences, and the greater access to different traditions made possible by the media.

The Church of England has had its own Head of Research and Statistics, itself an interesting reflection of where its attention lies, and she has produced useful summaries of the current research (Barley 2006). One of the problems with this survey approach is that of knowing what people mean by the answers they give, but accepting that limitation, they do provide a degree of objectivity and a guide to changes and trends.

It is to be noted first of all that belief in God, especially a personal God, is declining, according to these statistics. In 1968, 77 per cent of the population in Britain said they believed in God, but 35 years later this figure had fallen to 67 per cent. Belief in a personal God had fallen even further, from 45 per cent in 1968 to 26 per cent in 2000. Results from a range of surveys such as the National Centre for Social Research, ICM and MORI Ltd have yielded broadly similar figures, so one might safely assume that this is indeed a general trend. Other supposedly traditional beliefs, such as that in heaven and hell, the existence of sin and the devil, have remained more constant. Interestingly, belief in a human soul has increased over the same period of time, and this might suggest a heightened concern for individual rather than collective spirituality, but one must beware of reading too much into this without other evidence.

The most significant finding, however, relates to people's sense of spiritual awareness, which is definitely on the increase. It may be that it is now more acceptable to admit to such experiences as the culture shifts towards a greater sensitivity to the personal and subjective, and it is interesting to note recent TV programmes such as *The Monastery* and *The Retreat* that focus on individuals pursuing their spiritual journey through encounters with the more esoteric versions of traditional faiths. The first of these programmes saw a group of people entering a Roman Catholic Order's pattern of religious life for a limited period of time. The second was based in an Islamic setting in Spain. That such programmes now make good TV is itself a measure of the growing interest in spirituality, although again one must be cautious about how this might differ from traditional understandings.

According to research carried out for the BBC's *Soul of Britain* programme made in 2000, 76 per cent of people are now likely to admit to having a religious or spiritual experience, compared to a figure of 48 per cent in 1987. Thirty-eight per cent claim to have experienced an awareness of the presence of God and a similar number to have felt help in answering prayer (Barley 2006: 4). Interestingly Estate Agents have recorded that about half of potential homebuyers believe in ghosts and a MORI poll revealed that 38 per cent thought they had had a personal experience of this. As has already been suggested, it is difficult to know to what extent this simply reflects a changing general culture in which it is now more acceptable to talk about and acknowledge such things, or whether these are actual increases in the numbers claiming such experiences. The concept of a plausibility structure, coined by Peter Berger a sociologist of religion (Berger 1967), seems helpful in this context. If the surrounding frameworks of interpretation allow or acknowledge the existence of specific beliefs and their practical manifestation, then it is much more likely that these will be publicly articulated and recorded. If, however, such beliefs are not part of public discourse, then it becomes much more difficult to interpret events and experiences in this particular way and less likely that people will see them as examples of the belief let alone be prepared to talk openly about them. So perhaps plausibility structures have begun to change, and it is that which needs addressing and interpreting as much as the empirical evidence.

Does any of this translate into church attendance? This is where the disjunction between the revived spirituality and traditional forms of religion begins to appear. There is no evidence that this renewed spiritual awareness is leading to increased religious affiliation. In fact, people are more likely to admit to being spiritual than they are to being religious (31 per cent as against 27 per cent in one poll). This is perhaps the most important aspect of the research. Barley concludes:

> Modern Britain embraces spirituality but sees no need to align itself with any formalized religion or faith community … Indeed for many people today it is a Godless spirituality, a consumer-driven pick 'n' mix approach to spirituality or an inherited folk religion that is becoming acceptable, perhaps even fashionable. They see no need to conform to a single religious framework and no conflict in adopting belief systems according to individual preferences. (Barley 2006: 5)

Once again we appear to be confronted with the classic symptoms or characteristics of the influences of a globalized culture. An unwillingness to engage with the institutions that have hitherto sustained and reproduced the beliefs and practices in question, and the subsequent disembedding of the beliefs from stable communities and localities; the emphasis upon individual choice and preference that appears to reflect a consumerist and commodity-based approach to life generally; the blurring of boundaries between the different traditions and religious resources that suggest these are now becoming zombie categories, even though they still appear in familiar forms. Above all, perhaps, it suggests that religion or spirituality is becoming just one more resource for individual identity construction, subject no longer to the constraints of wider faith communities and their disciplines, but rather to the current needs and requirements of individuals as they struggle for meaning or personal space within a commercially driven culture that throws them back on their own resources. So people hunt around for what might help them survive the rigours of employment and family in the global economy, and offer them psychological support and even an escape, adopting what is of obvious and immediate benefit to them, but rejecting or abandoning what is not of any apparent value in their 'personal journey'. This is that much easier now that one can access anything through the internet and one can find a group of like-minded people in most centres of population pursuing similar aims.

What is practical theology to make of this? What are the implications not just for those who now seek their spiritual fulfilment beyond the traditional churches, but also for those either left behind in the pews, or who do attend church events but perhaps with an unfamiliar mind-set and non-traditional expectations? Does Christianity knowingly or unknowingly start to take on some of the characteristics of this new religious culture and, if so, is that a problem?

The Kendal Project

Before these questions can be addressed it is important to move beyond the quantitative approach to these changes presented by Barley to examine a more qualitative one that highlights exactly the issues identified above. A team from Lancaster University has conducted an in-depth piece of research in the town of Kendal in the English Lake District (Heelas and Woodhead 2005). Their objective was to test out the thesis that there is now a spiritual revolution taking place, and to see whether or not what have hitherto been seen as alternative approaches by traditional faith communities are challenging the established faith in terms of both numbers and credibility.

Although the team's findings are of interest, the concentration will be upon the interpretations of the results, and the frameworks that are used to explain what was found. The key suggested to understanding what is happening, they describe as the 'subjective turn' (Heelas and Woodhead 2005: 2). What do they mean by this?

> 'The turn' is shorthand for a major cultural shift of which we all have some experience. It is a turn away from life lived in terms of external or 'objective' roles, duties and obligations, and a turn towards life lived by reference to one's own subjective experiences (relational as much as individualistic) … The subjective turn is thus a turn away from 'life-as' (life lived as a dutiful wife, father, husband, strong leader, self-made man etc.) to 'subjective life' (life lived in deep connection with the unique experiences of my self in-relation). (Heelas and Woodhead 2005: 2–3)

This is about other forms of disembedding, not just from specific locality and tradition, but also from roles that one is likely to play and the obligations that go with them. Rather than an emphasis upon the external demands upon one's life there is a concentration upon individual states of consciousness, states of mind, memories, emotions, bodily experiences and inner conscience. Constructing one's own identity and sense of self in such a way that well-being and peace of mind are achieved become the true objectives of the spiritual journey. One might argue that evidence of this is now available in the sphere of marriage, where the emphasis is no longer on the importance of honouring and maintaining the institution of marriage within society, but instead upon what the individuals concerned get out of and put into the relationship. The 'so what is in it for me' approach becomes the real focus of attention.

The claims that were investigated in the Kendal project were these. That 'life-as' forms of the sacred, which emphasize a transcendent source of significance and authority and which outweigh personal needs and considerations, are likely to be in decline, and that 'subjective-life' forms of the sacred, drawing upon those inner resources as signs of meaning, are likely to be on the increase. In order to establish whether or not this is the case the researchers investigated not only the traditional congregations in the town but also many other so-called 'alternative' groups with whom they could make contact. The list of these 'holistic milieu activities' in and around 5 miles of Kendal ranged from the more obvious groups such as Yoga and Reflexology to the Wild Women Group and Play Therapy (Heelas and Woodhead 2005: 156–7). One of the conclusions is that most of these latter groups can no longer be described as 'alternative' at all, simply because they have become part of a new 'establishment', and an accepted part of life within the general culture.

Another question is the extent to which these varied activities can really be described as spirituality. The authors are well aware of this, and questioned the people involved as to how they themselves interpreted what it is they are engaged in. It is clear that the whole debate becomes quite complex because there is no agreed definition of the term, and imposing a traditional interpretation would miss the point of the research. Another related and important issue is the slippage that occurs between a practice and set of beliefs that have been derived from an identifiable religious tradition, and yet are being presented in a manner that can be quite distant and remote from these origins. The most obvious example is perhaps yoga, which can be practised without reference to its origins. But that illustrates the change that is at the heart of this discussion. Authority no longer stems from a tradition as such, policed by its officials and teachers, but only from within the individual who becomes their own arbiter of what is of value and significance as they 'mine' the resources of various traditions.

The Subjectivization Thesis

As stated earlier, it is less the actual findings of the research than the framework by which it is interpreted, that is of value for practical theology. It needs to be noted that the figures from Kendal suggested that the 'alternatives' had not yet overtaken the traditional religious groups, although if current trends continued this might occur at some point in the future. One of the difficulties is that of knowing how many people attend both sorts of activity. There is anecdotal evidence that regular church-goers also attend other groups but are unwilling to admit this to their clergy for fear of being reprimanded in some way or of appearing disloyal or uncommitted. They get their regular dose of formal religion and congregational life at church but their more spiritual needs are met elsewhere. If this is the case, then it becomes harder to evaluate the figures which might reflect more of a redistribution or duplication than a real increase overall. It also raises the question of what is missing from normal church life, and whether or how that might be addressed within the more formal setting.

The main thrust of the thesis is that meaning is now derived from the internal and subjective rather than from the external and traditional practice and beliefs of faith communities. Although some of this stems from the writing of the sociologist Durkheim, the authors draw heavily upon more recent research from the World Values Survey and its interpretation by Ronald Inglehart (Heelas and Woodhead 2005: 79). Inglehart has identified what he calls 'post-materialist' values, which are now increasingly prevalent across the globe, and these relate to concerns for self-expression and personal well-being. The argument is that these newer values have not yet overtaken materialistic ones, but that they are on the increase and are becoming more significant. They are to be found not only in the obvious religious settings, but also in the spheres of education, business and health care. Being 'true to oneself' or cultivating 'emotional or spiritual intelligence' are familiar phrases within the discourses of these professions. An emphasis upon personal development as an aspect of professional development or performance management is established within the human resource field. So learning to 'manage oneself', and one's emotions, becomes a central task in adapting to contemporary life and its pressures, and replaces the idea that one can behave appropriately by conforming to some external code of practice or religious belief structure.

The term that is coming to the fore and to which practical theology must give more attention is 'well-being'. Whilst one must be wary of the latest fashion and attempt to establish critical perspectives on the growth of this discourse, it is necessary also to respect and understand what lies behind this. To what extent does it become just another marketing ploy encouraging people to consume certain goods and services that are argued to contribute to one's individual well-being, or are there some criteria by which one might evaluate current practice and vision within economic and political life? These are questions that will be addressed in a later chapter but they arise naturally from this concern with spirituality.

Heelas and Woodhead argue that what they have described as the 'holistic milieu', encountered in the alternative approach to spirituality, fits into this wider cultural shift. It is the unique and individual that is the focus of these activities. Yet these are important because they contribute to more effective or satisfying relationships, whether in one's personal life or at work. However, the field of spiritual development must not be reduced to the debate about subjective well-being as it still contains elements that relate to something beyond the individual and may act as the basis for a critique of what happens within this cultural shift.

At this point it is important to express reservations about the Kendal thesis. One needs to be wary of employing a single framework of interpretation to explain what is a complex and essentially blurred set of processes. I would suggest that to attribute the growth in interest in matters spiritual solely to the subjectivist turn as identified from within the surrounding culture, might be to miss other important aspects of what is happening. The test of this will presumably come when the current fashion of focusing upon personal development within other disciplines begins to fade and as the critique of this as being subject to and determined by commercial and financial pressures becomes more established. Will individuals continue to pursue their own spiritual journey drawing upon the resources available from a plurality of religious traditions even if this no longer fits neatly into a portfolio approach to identity construction in the discourse of professional development? I suspect that they will, because it is about deeper needs and demands.

The other major question is that of how practical theology might evaluate these developments within spirituality and the extent to which it might encourage Christians to engage with them. Does the Christian tradition have its own understanding of well-being that could form the basis for a critical view of the wider cultural shift or does it have something distinctive to contribute to the general debate? What is an 'authentic spirituality' and what is to be considered a questionable set of developments that appear to be shaped and determined by external (global) forces that need to be brought into question? Whilst one may not agree with Cavanaugh's answer to this question, it is nevertheless a legitimate one to raise. Is such a movement within spirituality no more than another example of the enclosure entailed by globalization and a means of entrapment by specific economic forces and interests, or does it have the capacity to act as a critique of these? Before addressing these questions it will be necessary to examine another interpretation of what is happening in the field of spirituality.

Deregulation or Decline?

So far the vexed question of how to define spirituality has been put to one side, but it has to be acknowledged that this discussion is dominated by an underlying concept of the spiritual life which identifies it with the practices and beliefs of settled religious communities. However, if it is exactly such a social context that, it is argued, is beginning to change, then it could be that one is reviewing developments and prospects using an inappropriate and outdated conceptual framework. Rather than suggesting that current developments in spirituality should be evaluated against the criteria from this previous period, perhaps the recent changes need to be understood in their own right and by employing different categories. What is important is not whether or not what is new corresponds to the self-understanding and structures of what has gone before, but whether it has its own internal validity and integrity. It is just such an approach that is to be encountered in the work of Christopher Partridge and offers a challenging and distinctive slant which moves beyond that of Heelas and Woodhead (Partridge 2004).

As an example of this one can take analyses of what is called 'New Age' religion and examine the terms in which these have been carried out. Partridge refers in depth to the work of Steve Bruce (Bruce 2003) who is a leading sociologist of religion and major contributor to recent debates on secularization.

Bruce argues that this emerging form of 'diffuse religion', very much the type of activities identified by the Kendal project, is essentially precarious and unlikely to lead to long-term secure developments for a number of related reasons. Because it does not submit itself to a central authority but depends rather upon the individual, it is difficult to translate it into any stable form of social order. A number of other difficulties then arise from this. In a consumer-orientated culture, religion is in danger of becoming no more than a commodity that is chosen or rejected on the grounds of whether or not it benefits one's individual spiritual journey. This means that there is no orthodoxy or orthopraxis that will emerge and help to control and sustain further coherent development. Bruce believes that belief systems require such social structures in order to survive over time. New Age type beliefs and practices will not be around indefinitely because there is not enough infrastructure to hold people together. It must be recognized that it is easy for committed Christians to agree with this judgement because their experience of religion runs counter to that of the New Age and presupposes settled faith communities and centrally controlled order.

There is also an assumption that local groups of faith adherents provide a sort of community pressure that itself generates cohesion and agreement, but that this will be lacking in the newer forms of spirituality. Where there is nobody of authority holding the belief system together, whether locally or more widely, Bruce suggests, and I suspect many Christians would concur, there can be no coherent or identifiable system to make claims upon people's allegiance or to provide a means of passing on the teaching to others. But is this in fact a new type of religious movement that does not require the same sort of structures as traditional religion?

A further concern is that New Age spiritualities have no real social impact or political cutting edge. Unlike many Christian reformers down the ages there is, as yet anyway, little evidence that these new forms of spirituality offer people the motivation or support to become involved in counter-cultural issues, albeit that some are already wrapped up in environmental concerns. Bruce considers it unlikely that schools, housing association, women's refuges or urban renewal programmes will emerge from within the New Age movement.

Perhaps the most significant criticism though is that these alternative spiritualities are simply conformist in that they offer individuals ways in which they can cope with the stresses and strains of modern life, survival techniques perhaps, but that this is to trivialize even those practices which are adopted from the formal faith traditions. Meditation, for instance, is seen as a useful technique when responding to external work or domestic pressures, but really has no deeper meaning or purpose. People's lives will not be transformed nor their life-styles challenged, but they will be made slightly more comfortable in order that as little as possible has to be changed. Alongside this there will be no need to go out to make converts or to evangelize, as individuals are expected to make their own personal path through the options available, and to construct their own personalized package of useful spiritual techniques and beliefs.

> To conclude, alternative spiritualities provide eclectic, individualized religion for disenchanted Westerners who want to hang onto the remnants of belief without inconveniencing themselves too much. Such religion does not claim absolute truth, does not require devotion to one religious leader, does not insist on the authority of a single set of sacred writings, but rather encourages exploration, eclecticism, an understanding of the self as divine, and, consequently, often a belief in the final authority only of the self. (Partridge 2004: 36)

This is not Partridge's own view, as will be seen in a moment, but summarizes Bruce's interpretation and probably agrees with the type of judgement that many Christians would make from within their own stable and settled context. If they are correct of course it merely supports Bruce's interpretation as a sociologist that the New Age movement is part of the continuing decline of religion and the process of secularization. So all the figures quoted earlier about a widening interest in spirituality would be of no comfort whatsoever to traditional Christians or to practical theology. They would rather confirm that orthodox beliefs and practices are in decline and that the supposed substitutes for them that might appear superficially attractive to churches that wanted to adapt and bring themselves up-to-date are really a dead end and a distraction. So agreeing with Bruce is, in fact, a double-edged sword.

What is Partridge's alternative interpretation and does it hold out any greater hope for traditional Christianity? He argues that what one encounters is deregulation rather than decline, and that this is less secularization and more a relocation of religion (Partridge 2004: 39). One of the problems with views such as those of Bruce is that they reflect the values and social position of a global elite (mainly academics) who are unable to give proper credibility to the new movements in spirituality. This is because they are using the wrong tools to interpret what is happening and view recent developments through the lenses provided by academia and their own specific secularized versions of reality. They are unable therefore to give proper attention to the emerging and detraditionalized forms of popular spirituality. Religion is not disappearing but reconfiguring in ways that neither traditional believers nor their anti-religious academic counterparts can recognize.

Partridge coins the term 'occulture' to describe what he believes is happening. This is a new culture of dissent and opposition based more upon forms of what have previously been called 'magic' by the intellectual elites. As people turn away from formal and institutional religion, so they move instead into a different sort of re-enchantment of the world, one which is not only an obvious reaction against the secular values of a global culture, but which also exhibits a genuine striving for the spiritual and the supernatural. So there is a return to the sacred, but not one that holds out any great hope for some sort of reconciliation with, or accommodation to, more orthodox religious beliefs. Those who now study contemporary forms of religious expression and spirituality need to shed their traditionalist-dominated frameworks of interpretation and assumptions and recognize the new movements on their own terms and as representing genuinely new forms of religious life.

Whether or not one agrees with Partridge, and he provides much evidence to back up his argument, one can see that his interpretation launches an interesting challenge to practical theology. If he is correct, it would be very dangerous and potentially undermining of traditional Christianity to engage in a significant blurring of boundaries with the developing spiritualities as they represent an almost alien approach to religion. They may indeed suggest that this is about a deregulation rather than a decline of religion, but how could an established church structure of belief and practice encompass such freedom and individual choice within its confines? Without some authority system agreed and accepted by most of its adherents the institutional church would surely descend into anarchy? Yet if he is wrong, the figures suggest that a continued process of secularization, as argued by scholars such as Bruce, is what is happening, and practical theology will find itself increasingly marginalized and restricted to an ageing traditionalist constituency.

If both Bruce and Partridge are correct in their views it would seem that any attempt by Christians to absorb or adapt themselves to the new forms of spirituality, to blur the boundaries in some way, would be a mistake. According to Bruce, this would represent allowing inside the walls the Trojan horse of a consumerist mentality that erodes real commitment, let alone any social or political critique. If Partridge is right, then the Trojan horse would effect the undermining of any notion of authority or orthodoxy within the Christian tradition, and bring in a 'free-for-all' based upon the turn to subjectivization that Heelas and Woodhead describe. Nothing but damage could result from any sort of accommodation with these globally influenced and shaped versions of the spiritual life. Unless it is possible to present an alternative interpretation of the alternative spiritualities themselves then one cannot see how they can be anything but a disaster for traditional Christianity.

Challenging the Authority of Tradition

It is becoming clear from these arguments that the central issue is how attitudes towards tradition have been changed and undermined by the influences of globalization. Both Heelas and Woodhead's concept of subjectivization and Partridge's notion of the deregulation of spirituality bring to the surface the fact that it is individuals who now make supposedly autonomous choices, rather than the frameworks provided by institutions that determine how contemporary spiritualities are formed in the market place of a plurality of religious resources. What is less clear is whether practical theology in its task of creating a critically engaged Christian praxis can legitimately work within this new situation, or whether it must reject such a possibility and remain within the confines of what can be described as a traditional approach to tradition. Until this has been established it is impossible to decide how Christianity might move forward in its engagement with new and developing spiritualities.

The concept of reflexivity will come into the equation in due course, but before this can happen it is necessary to examine potential frameworks for interpreting what is often termed detraditionalization or living in a post-traditional society (Beck, Giddens and Lash 1994: ch. 2). Giddens himself offers an important way into this debate and it is his argument that will be pursued first.

Although globalization can be viewed solely as an external phenomenon concerned only with economic and political matters, Giddens suggests that a sociological approach requires a deeper level of analysis, including investigating the subjective and intimate aspects of people's lives. Echoing themes encountered in previous chapters, he states that the disembedding of individuals from the context of community and locality will change the dynamic of personal and intimate relationships. The reason for this is that globalization changes the ways in which time and space are controlled and managed. Tradition has shaped space through its control of time whereas globalization does the opposite because it is essentially 'action at a distance' within which absence predominates over presence as space itself is reconfigured (Beck, Giddens and Lash 1994: 96).

The practical impact of this is that traditions which were previously able to remain distinct from others because contact was so limited, now have to face regular encounters with other traditions. Giddens says that this post-traditional society is the first global society:

> Until relatively recently, much of the world remained in a quasi-segmental state, in which many large enclaves of traditionalism persisted. In these areas, and also in some regions and contexts of the more industrially developed countries, the local community continued to be strong. Over the past few decades particularly influenced by the development of instantaneous global electronic communication, these circumstances have altered in a radical way. A world where no one is 'outside' is one where pre-existing traditions cannot avoid contact not only with others but also with many alternative ways of life. By the same token, it is one where the 'other' cannot any longer be treated as inert. (Beck, Giddens and Lash 1994: 96–7)

One can recognize this from the research carried out by the Kendal project and the proliferation of different holistic and religious approaches now co-existing within the same small locality. From within this menu of possibilities individuals are now free to select, adopt and then, if it no longer suits, abandon, any one or a mixture of these traditions. Thus the very nature of the relationship with traditions changes.

It is not that traditions disappear – like zombie categories they remain and appear to be unchanged – but there are then two possibilities, according to Giddens. Either they submit themselves to discursive articulation and defence, thus having to be justified alongside or in competition with the other available traditions, or else they turn their backs on such dialogue and become instead forms of fundamentalism. So even the apparent strict and uncritical adherence to a tradition, which might have been the only option when no other traditions were available, becomes a positive and deliberate choice. One chooses not to choose, but with the knowledge that one could have made a very different choice.

This has particular significance for religion, as it is clearly identified with conferring authority upon traditions through its connection with the sacred. Once one invests the past with a divine presence, then any related practices and rituals have a religious quality, and truth tends to be presented in a formula which immunizes the tradition from challenge. So it is more than simply 'this is the way things have always been done' because there is a deeper level of justification and legitimation underlying it. However, the link with the sacred also comes under threat through globalization as religious traditions themselves lose their unassailable authority.

The fundamental change that practical theology must be aware of is that any tradition must now engage with others through a process of articulation and dialogue, if it is to present itself as worthy of attention. If it rejects this option then it becomes a form of fundamentalism which may claim to be simply a traditional approach to tradition but cannot be such because it too is now a matter of choice. It is at this point that the notion of reflexivity begins to emerge, as this is the term that is used to describe the process whereby individuals make these choices. So any contemporary spirituality would be seen to be a reflexive spirituality, whether or not the choice made is to remain within the Christian tradition or to construct a more eclectic product. It needs to be seen how this understanding is itself linked to a version of social evolution that will progress our wider discussion of spirituality.

Reflexivity in the Context of Social Evolution

This is the heart of the argument, and demands a full exposition if its implications, not only for worship and spirituality, but also for all the other categories of practical theology. In order to illustrate this I return briefly to a comment made by the Head of Research and Statistics at the Church of England. Commenting on how the established churches might respond to the apparent flowering of alternative spiritualities she says: ‘the church has foundations of faith that mean it cannot act as a spiritual supermarket where people make their own selections of belief’ (Barley 2006: 14). There are two inescapable responses to this that summarize precisely how and why practical theology must accept that it is in danger of being restricted to zombie categories. First, whether the church likes it or not, people make their own selections of belief, and even those who choose to remain within the traditional patterns of belief and practice do so as a matter of positive decision. Second, what lies behind this is far more profound a change than Barley acknowledges by simply describing it as a ‘spiritual supermarket’. What is becoming clear is that selecting belief cannot be reduced to a consumer model but is the consequence of a significant development and shift within the wider culture. As Giddens suggests, it is the open encounter with other traditions that forces each single tradition to articulate and defend its own beliefs. This bringing of religious beliefs into the public forum can only be done through language. This is the most important change that has occurred in recent generations and leads directly into the subject of reflexivity.

In order to grasp this it is necessary to make a brief examination of another sociologist and engaged political commentator, Habermas. Like Giddens he argues that it is this ‘turn to language’ that has changed the nature of traditions and leads to this point where individuals have no choice but to articulate and justify their belief positions in the forum of open debate. However, he places this in a wider discussion about the direction of social evolution, suggesting that this is indeed the place that the Western post-Enlightenment tradition has itself reached and that even though there can still be enclaves where traditions present themselves as being immune from this evolutionary process, this is largely self deception. No tradition, including Habermas’s own, can avoid the challenge to its self-understanding posed by the encounter with other traditions, and this forces each of us to consider why we should either remain within that tradition, or why we might abandon it and perhaps establish allegiance to another. This requires us to exercise reflexivity, a process of increased critical self-awareness and an articulation of where we stand and why.

Habermas describes this movement as ‘the linguistification of the sacred’ and bases upon it his own ‘theory of communicative reason’ (1987: 146). In simple terms, in a previous era, when traditions or ways of life were more self-enclosed, religions played a significant role in binding societies together and providing the structures of social life. They could do this because their position as frameworks of interpretation was unchallenged and there were no real alternatives available. Now this has been broken down by the impact of modernity and the encounter with other traditions, the authority of any one tradition can no longer be taken for granted. Each must justify itself, if possible, at the bar of open debate and dialogue.

It needs to be recognized that Habermas does not present this as some sort of irrevocable process that has already forced its way unnoticed into our intellectual culture, but that it leads instead to a sort of fragmented consciousness where the remnants of the original traditions still appear in apparently familiar forms, but alongside newly reflexive traditions that are struggling to come to terms with these new demands. Very much like Beck, he acknowledges that adherence to belief systems will continue in ways that, on the surface of it, can legitimately claim that nothing has changed. The fact that these are zombie categories which are being challenged and undermined by a social evolution often remains unnoticed. One might add that the changes are now being noticed by commentators like Barley within the Christian tradition, but they offer a simplistic explanation for them that fails to recognize their profound nature, hence they argue that the tradition can retain its old-style authority and needs only to stand firm in the face of a consumerist mentality. The foundations – to use Barley's own terms – have been well and truly shaken – which is not to say that the Christian tradition has no future, but rather that the future is more likely to be along the path of a greater articulation and defence of its beliefs and the exercise of reflexivity, or a critical and questioning self-awareness by its individual adherents. This leads naturally to an examination of whether forms of reflexive spirituality can be identified in current Christian belief and practice.

Chapter 5

Reflexive Spirituality and Globalization

Is it possible to identify what a reflexive spirituality might look like, one that moves the Christian tradition forward into its global context while not compromising the integrity of the tradition? In order to examine this question it is necessary to see how spirituality can itself become the subject of critical study.

The Study of the Human Spirit

This appears at first sight to be both an impossibly ambitious enterprise and also one that might resist any attempts at academic study. Surely spirituality is not something to be studied or objectified but rather something that we are either engaged in or simply aware of. Even more than religion or theology, it is about practice rather than structures of belief that lend themselves to analysis or categorization. One has to recognize the understandable and even justifiable resistance to treating spirituality as another subject to be studied and discussed. There are however significant works devoted to this, including writings from within the field itself, for instance, Evelyn Underhill's classic text *Mysticism: The Nature and Development of Spiritual Consciousness* (1993). In theory there is no reason why this aspect of human behaviour should not be open to critical investigation, or why such investigation should not prove illuminating for those who practise spirituality as well as for those who wish to study it. The argument is that globalization, with its blurring of boundaries and frequent crossing of thresholds, requires a greater degree of self-awareness and understanding of this dimension of human activity. If reflexivity is a characteristic of the global or cosmopolitanized era, then it is likely that there will emerge forms of reflexive spirituality. What we learn about our own behaviour and processes of belief will itself inform what spirituality might become and directions in which it will develop.

I have used elsewhere a distinction suggested by the philosopher Levinas in order to help us see what is going on here (Reader 2005). Levinas talks about the difference between 'the Saying and the Said'. The Saying is the direct personal experience or encounter (with God) that resists all attempts to articulate let alone codify or analyse what is going on. The oft-quoted example would be God's demand of Abraham that he sacrifice his son Isaac – an action that could be neither described nor justified according to any system of ethics or even from within his own faith. Abraham either obeyed the call or had to decide to ignore it. Had he gone through with the command, which he was prepared to do, he would have been left with no means of articulating this action and its justification to his own family, let alone to anybody else. Yet the Saying always has to be turned into the Said, put into the form of description or analysis as soon as it needs to be communicated to another human being. Can one witness in silence? Once the silence is broken then the full depth and meaning of the Saying slips through the net because it is simply impossible to do justice to the reality of the direct encounter or experience. This is also true of other profound aspects of human experience, such as falling in love. This is to acknowledge the limits and constraints of language whilst also to recognize that communication leaves us little choice but to reduce the Saying to the Said. Yet within the Said there is invariably a residue of the Saying which both haunts and challenges every instance of the Said. The one never finally eclipses the other.

There is a constant process of struggle towards articulation which is immediately drawn back into its impossibility by the knowledge of the limits of the human capacity to describe or analyse – an inescapable tension with which those of faith just have to live. If spirituality is about such direct experiences then it is to be expected that all attempts to put these into language should carry a health warning, yet without those attempts there could be no tradition or communication of the insights and visions of spirituality. There has to be both the Saying and the Said. This may help us come to terms with the necessity for and the limits of the study and analysis of spirituality.

There is a further argument which reminds us that spirituality is a dimension of human consciousness, and that, in itself, is a vital and constantly developing area of human exploration. What does it mean to be human? Are there other possibilities of which we are only yet dimly aware and of which spiritual awareness might be the 'tip of the iceberg'? In case this too should sound unlikely I draw attention to a recent publication in which the Dalai Lama was in conversation with a number of scientists specializing in human behaviour, which were reported by Daniel Goleman who is well known for his work on emotional intelligence (Goleman 2004). This includes reports of a neurological study of Buddhist monks who claim to have reached deeper levels of consciousness through the practice of meditation. The work of Antonio Damasio (2000), a US based neuroscientist, is also worth mentioning in this context, in particular his investigations into how what he calls the emotions are related in the brain to the areas normally associated with human reasoning, and how damage to the one also impairs the functioning of the other. Studies of heightened levels of consciousness have also been written from within the Christian tradition, for instance David Granfield's *Heightened Consciousness: The Mystical Difference* (1991). All of which is to point out that such studies do exist and that they form a growing corpus of work on the subject of spirituality. They look set to come up with interesting and significant findings.

This is crucial for the argument because it suggests that not all manifestations of what are currently counted as spirituality are to be taken at face value or to be considered self-authenticating or self-validating. Merely to label a particular practice or set of beliefs as spirituality does not render them immune from critique or rigorous examination. There is a temptation to talk about this subject as some form of mysticism and to suggest therefore that this places it beyond study or reflection. Not everything that passes as spirituality necessarily justifies being accepted or respected, certainly not uncritically.

A recent example of a feminist critique of the Christian mystical tradition is Grace Jantzen's *Power, Gender and Christian Mysticism* (1995). One of the problems with such an approach, as Jantzen herself acknowledges, is that if one takes a particular perspective from which to critique the tradition on the grounds that it is not to be uncritically validated, then that basis of critique itself cannot be granted an uncritical validation, it is simply one perspective and others might claim to be equally valid. Where could there be 'solid ground' from which to launch a critical examination into the subject of spirituality? According to what criteria could one argue that spirituality X is superior to or more appropriate than spirituality Y? As Jantzen says in her conclusion:

> Is the mystical a social construction all the way down, or is there some 'real' or 'true' mysticism against which all others can be measured and to which it might be appropriate to aspire? (Jantzen 1995: 352)

The Work of Ken Wilber

Having laid out the territory and identified some of the problems, and in particular the crucial question of how to develop means of evaluating different spiritualities, I turn to the writer who has come closest so far to achieving this objective. Scholars from the Christian tradition may not have heard of Ken Wilber, although his work has been referred to recently in a couple of texts from within this faith context (Howard and Welbourne 2004; see also Fontana 2003). It is difficult to categorize his work, although one could describe it as a psychology of religion in its broadest sense, but Wilber's range and depth of knowledge of both different spiritual traditions and academic disciplines is beyond such a straightforward categorization. My own first encounter dates back to the late 1980s and the time when a number of us were trying to evaluate developments in Creation or Green spirituality.

Wilber was the first person I had read who was prepared to look critically at the ideas that were developing in an attempt to judge whether or not what was coming out of that movement, at the time, was progressive or regressive. A very powerful insight was his suggestion that some Green spirituality in fact represented a regression to an earlier stage of spiritual development, one which claimed to achieve a return to an undifferentiated vision of a sense of wholeness or unity with nature and which thereby failed to take into account elements of human intellectual and spiritual progress which included the exercise of human reason. Feelings of being at one with the natural world, which many experience from time to time, are not, in themselves, a sound or adequate basis for a developing spirituality, although they may be the trigger or starting point for spiritual development.

It will be clear from this that what lies behind Wilber's approach is an evolutionary or developmental understanding of human consciousness and spirituality, one which he documents and supports from a wealth of other sources. This, in itself, is controversial, but seems to me the most convincing candidate for a foundation for the construction of a critique of spiritualities.

I take as a starting point a footnote comment from one of Wilber's early books where he says: 'We are still awaiting the analyst who as brilliantly studies the distortions and oppressions of spirituality, the repression of transcendence, the politics of Tao, the denial of Being by beings' (Wilber 1983: 116).

Those few words require considerable unpacking and constitute a lifetime's work, probably for a group of people rather than any one individual, but it seems that Wilber himself has now set out on this trail. When he wrote that sentence he was talking about the ways in which Freud, Marx and then Habermas had identified the distortions that occur at different levels of human development. Freud had drawn out blocks and distortions at the emotional–sexual level; Marx at the material–economic level and Habermas at the level of communicative exchange. Wilber seeks to identify their equivalent at the level of spiritual development.

Using that framework I present my own developmental schema drawing upon some different sources, but also influenced by the ideas of Freud and Habermas. I suggest that there are four levels at which humans normally operate: the unconscious; practical consciousness – a sort of normal, everyday, just getting on with practical tasks in an unthinking way level; critical consciousness; and transpersonal consciousness (Reader 1994). The purpose and use of this is that it makes it possible to examine how humans operate and to judge at which level religious and spiritual development is taking place.

Much religious belief and practice might be seen to have been operating at the level of practical consciousness, until fairly recently – so what one believes is taken for granted and placed within a tradition to which one gives unquestioning adherence or obedience (the traditional approach to tradition). However, given the encounters with other traditions, let alone the challenges of science and other disciplines to religious belief, and the general undermining by the secular culture, that level will no longer suffice. Unless religion can come through and survive at the level of critical consciousness and learn to cope with the criticisms of religion emerging from these other sources, it will not be sustained with real conviction. It might continue as some sort of habit or practice of social bonding, but not have any deep spiritual or intellectual content. Yet simply to make religion subject to some external intellectual criteria which evolve from elsewhere is itself to distort spiritual insight – hence the level of the transpersonal which, in its turn, provides a critique of the critical consciousness. Globalization and reflexivity demand that religion at the very least reaches the level of critical consciousness, but that too needs to be transcended. (The post- or non-traditional approach to tradition is thus taken further). This gets complicated, so here is another attempt to articulate the same idea.

I reduce the four levels to three, using the notion of autonomy as the central theme (Reader 2005: 100–113), and, building upon the work of the philosopher Derrida, suggest that there is a level one might term pre-autonomy, which then develops into autonomy, followed by post-autonomy. The details of this are slightly different to the previous framework, but the intention is the same; to be able to evaluate what level of human operation is functioning at any one moment and to thus critique processes that are either not what they claim to be or that require further development. The post-autonomous level is inevitably the most elusive and difficult to describe but would point towards the deeper levels that are to be found in Wilber's rather more complex scheme. So it is to that which we turn.

Levels of Consciousness

Wilber's theory is that there are six levels of consciousness which can be identified in ascending order:

1. The material level, at which consciousness is identified exclusively with sense data, and the self and the physical body are seen as synonymous – failure to progress beyond this level means there will be no awareness of an underlying unity.
2. The vital level: this is when consciousness becomes aware of the self and the distinction between life and death. So life is valued and death seen as either a threat or a mystery.
3. The discriminative level: the consciousness begins to categorize objects and events encountered in experience and to recognize differences between the purely physical and the world of inner experience, thoughts and perhaps spirituality.
4. The ratiocinative level: at this point the self develops the capacity for analytical and rational thought and becomes capable of abstract thinking and advanced theory building.
5. The causal level: consciousness now experiences pure contentless awareness, so rather than being aware of something, consciousness is simply conscious of itself – this is to access the higher levels of awareness normally associated with meditation and spiritual practices.
6. The Brahmanic level: consciousness is aware of reality as a united field of energy in which the material world, the individual and the source of all life (God, Brahman or the Absolute) are in essence identical with each other.

Those familiar with the work of Jung, Piaget, Kohlberg, James Fowler and the theologians who have used these stages of cognitive, emotional and spiritual development will recognize the first four of these levels, but what Wilber does is to take these even further, building upon both empirical research into faith development and also using the ideas and practices from a variety of faiths.

The argument is that each stage is transcended as and when one moves through into the one beyond, but that the best of the previous stage is absorbed into what then follows. Distortions at each stage need to be worked through and left behind, hence the importance of the work of those such as Freud, Marx and Habermas who have identified these at the different stages of development.

Most people would believe or argue that they had achieved level 4, although regression remains a constant possibility, but levels 5 and 6 lie beyond the experience of a high proportion, except perhaps in rare moments of insight and deeper awareness. When discussing Green spiritualities it is critical to note that the deepest levels of spiritual development pass through and beyond what might be called the level of reason, thus transcending it, but not denying its value and role in the overall process. In my own terminology this would mean going through the levels of critical consciousness or autonomy to those of transpersonal consciousness or post-autonomy.

This may sound increasingly speculative and unfamiliar to those from within the Christian tradition, particularly if one is threatened by or uneasy with ideas from other faith traditions. However, if one is to develop a framework or set of criteria by which to evaluate developing spiritualities, I argue, something like this is going to be required. How is one to view religious positions that claim to have reached a higher level of development and yet still operate on the basis of the culture that is supposedly left behind? What about the blurring of boundaries that is now characteristic of religious experience in the context of globalization and where elements from a whole range of different sources are mixed together in previously unknown ways? It will not be possible to evaluate these exclusively from within the terms of one tradition.

In the 'salad bowl' that is globalized spirituality where apparently 'anything goes', how can one gain a critical perspective on what is presented unless there is a grasp of a more widely based understanding of the spiritual insights and practices of other faiths? This is not the same as arguing for some new world religion that takes the best of each and abandons the rest in a new synthesis that satisfies nobody, for Wilber's approach takes with utmost seriousness the internal self-understandings of the different traditions and builds from them a developmental framework that each could recognize from within their own tradition. Elements of Christian mysticism and spirituality are present in levels 5 and 6 although many Christians might well not have encountered them through the institutional structures.

How does this aid in the task of evaluating the spiritualities that are emerging in response to the global changes identified in earlier chapters? Wilber has now gone further, by suggesting that one can see the characteristics of the different stages and what signs one might look for in order to judge what progress is being made (Wilber 2000). He develops a different framework for this task, and this is not to be confused with the one just described. If his level 3 in this is taken as a starting point, here is a world where the meaning of life is determined by strict demarcation lines between what is right and wrong as dictated by access to laws and rules, probably backed up by an appeal to a hierarchical authority. This world is also most probably paternalistic and depends on social sanctions in order to maintain its control over individuals. An uncritical and unquestioning approach to authority is part of the approach so what we have termed a 'traditional view of tradition' is to be recognized here and currently reflected in what are called fundamentalist understandings of faith positions. 'Furious religion', or a faith built upon the identity of resistance as described by Castells both fit into this category. Belonging to the group and conforming to its norms without question are motivating factors and attractions.

Level 4 however takes a more critical stance on matters of faith and depends on a more discriminating approach to all aspects of reality, and is what one is more likely to see as a scientifically based understanding of the world. Individual judgement is expected, the exercise of autonomy is given greater weight, and the value of what can be calculated and measured comes into its own. This is the point at which globalization is instantly recognizable, where economy, politics and society are seen as distinct spheres of operation and where religion quickly becomes a matter of private taste and decision, more like another consumer good or lifestyle choice. The dangers, limitations and distortions of this have already been made clear. Despite the progress that has been made, this world is now facing significant risks that it seems to have no means of controlling or combating. Runaway global capitalism is the consequence of getting stuck at this level of development. Alternative spiritualities begin to emerge, often eclectic in nature and disembedded from the traditions from which they have evolved – the non-traditional approach to tradition is characteristic of this level.

Beyond this is a level 5 which Wilber describes as the emergence of the Green Era, or the stage of the sensitive self. Awareness of others and response to their needs, the value of networking rather than hierarchy, a freedom from dogma and religious authority, greater sensitivity towards the planet and other living creatures, self as open and capable of being creatively reshaped and the importance of dialogue – such are the signs of this level of development. Pluralistic relativism is one way of describing this approach and it is to be found in movements such as Greenpeace, deep ecology, ecofeminism, the World Council of Churches, Human Rights groups and the writings of philosophers such as Derrida and Foucault. One might describe this as the new liberal establishment as it has developed, particularly since the 1980s, but which has now started to run out of ideas as it gains political power and runs the risk of becoming merely the latest fashion. The danger of getting stuck at this level is that dissatisfaction and frustration begin to set in as the political objectives associated with this fail to deliver their promises and more people, especially those who feel excluded from level 4, revert to furious religion or political reaction as a result.

Wilber argues that what is now required is a leap of consciousness beyond level 5, one which builds upon the previous levels but also leaves behind their distortions and oppressive elements. He identifies a level 6 which he calls integrative and a level 7 known as holistic. These are clearly dependent upon spiritual development and a sense of the greater unity and wholeness of the created order, one where the barriers and divisions we draw in our minds are seen as exactly that, constructions due to previous levels of consciousness which have now served their purpose and will become destructive if not transcended. Internal and external, objective and subjective, reason and emotion, faith and science, all the dualisms now pervading our thinking will be seen as different moments of the same basic reality. Mystical thought from all faith traditions offers glimpses of this possibility but articulates them in different ways. For Wilber, these are the next developmental stages on the human journey and provide the criteria by which we can evaluate where we are now and how we must progress.

How this response of spirituality to globalization is to be interpreted will ultimately come down to how one stands in relation to one's own particular faith tradition. It might be interpreted as such a challenge to orthodoxy or purity that it is simply a step (or two) too far for most to travel. I would argue, however, that Wilber's framework offers an invaluable resource by which to understand what is happening, not just in the inner world of spirituality but also the outer world of globalization, itself the product of levels 4 and 5. Green spirituality is acknowledged as being a vital stage along the way, but not itself the end of the journey. Versions of it need to be viewed critically as they are subject to the distortions that occur at every level, and perhaps this is the immediate task facing those who view the consequences of an unfettered global capitalism with increasing concern, but believe that the solutions lie not in saving the planet as such, but through the exploration of human consciousness and spirituality.

Chapter 6

Families, Children and Globalization

Introduction

Work with children and families still forms a familiar part of the portfolio of practical theology, although the concentration has tended to be on how to educate and bring young people up within the Christian tradition. So such issues as confirmation and the admission of unconfirmed church-going youngsters to Holy Communion have been at the forefront of internal church discussions in recent years. All-age worship and how to tailor regular patterns of worship generally to a younger age group have also dominated the field but with a background of an increased understanding of child development and what is appropriate for different age groups. Increasing numbers of adult confirmation candidates have perhaps shifted the debate away from the traditional confirmation classes for early teenagers, although this remains an established aspect of life in many churches.

I will argue however in this chapter that there is a much wider sphere of concern with which practical theology should engage and that an examination of this will throw light upon how congregations might play a more active role in current discussions about family life and relationships, all of this within the context of how global forces are now impacting upon what is still seen as the basic unit of human social existence and the setting within which our lives are shaped and formed. Do Christians fully understand the significance of the work that they are doing in this area, or is it simply a matter of getting younger people into church so that the older generations can feel that the traditions and structures which they value will be carried on by future generations? It has to be said that it often feels as though the anxiety of those who now inhabit the church that they will be the 'end of the line' is really the dominant factor behind much attempted church-based young people's work, rather than a real concern for and understanding of what the Christian faith might have to offer to families and children in a globalized world. Somewhat like current government agendas which seem more concerned with providing childcare so that more women can become economically active rather than with the direct interests of the child, church-based work is in danger of becoming merely instrumental – a means to the end of keeping the church going.

The Global Context of Family Life

A recent report from UNICEF (2007) draws out quite clearly how and why global issues are at the forefront of concerns about families and children. Whilst acknowledging that the research on this is still at the early stages, there is no doubt that this is an area that requires further attention. In theory every nation signs up to the idea that child survival and development are ethical imperatives, but their practice is varied to say the least. There are major differences between different countries depending upon such factors as geography, economic and political stability, let alone differing social and cultural values, hence generalizations are to be treated with caution.

As the new century enters the latter part of its first decade, it would seem that the hoped-for global growth in world markets, driven by rapid technological progress, has only occurred in and benefited certain parts of the globe. The report suggests that steady improvements in growth, household incomes and child well-being are generated in countries with robust human and physical infrastructure, reasonable social policies, prudent macroeconomic policies and free access to foreign markets. Where all of these have not been in place, opening up to the world economy has adversely affected child growth and well-being. Not only have things not improved as a result of globalization, they have indeed deteriorated. The result is that only a proportion of the world's children will benefit from globalization. The report argues that the opening up of markets is vital, but that it needs to be combined with appropriate and adequate social welfare infrastructure and the capacity of families to adapt to rapid social and economic change.

Clearly there are continued major concerns about the plight of children in poorer countries which are starting from a low economic base and already face significant problems which global forces can only exacerbate unless compensatory measures are taken. One might argue that these are legitimate areas of attention for practical theology as it attempts to work out how Christian principles of justice, poverty reduction and appropriate distribution of the goods of society are put into practice – or not – across the globe. Access to basic resources, water, warmth, vaccines and health care, education and employment opportunities for parents is likely to be at the top of the agenda in many countries. Under what political conditions are these going to be addressed and alleviated by the growth of the global economy and what are the factors that might inhibit or damage further child and family development? This is one major aspect in which globalization has a direct impact upon practical theology's concerns for the well-being of children and families.

Without in any way underestimating the significance of this range of issues, however, my intention in this chapter is to focus more clearly on the impact of globalization upon families and children in the more affluent Western countries, which already have a stronger economic base and where social welfare policies are more deeply embedded even though sometimes heavily politically contested. But before doing this it is important to offer some figures to support the argument that, in all countries, whatever their economic strength or otherwise, there are causes for concern. For this I draw upon a recent text written by a Harvard-based researcher who has carried out ground-breaking work in this area (Heymann 2007).

Having analysed surveys of 55,000 people from around the world, including over 1,000 in-depth interviews in over 160 nations, this book offers a disturbing overview of the current shape of family life. Amongst its key findings are that an estimated 930 million children under the age of 15 are being raised in households where all the adults work. Thirty-six per cent of the families interviewed had left a young child home alone and 39 per cent had left a sick child home alone or sent the child to school despite being ill. Clearly economic pressures are central to this and the surveys showed that 67 per cent of parents with an income of under $10 a day had to choose between losing pay and leaving a sick child at home. When this happens there seems to be a 2 in 3 chance that the child will suffer an accident or some other form of emergency. This in turn tends to lead to later behavioural or developmental problems. Nearly 1 in 4 of the parents interviewed took the children to work instead, often into unsafe and inappropriate environments.

Access to formal childcare is one supposed solution to these problems, but this depends upon a series of factors even within more developed countries and raises further questions about the impact of this upon child development. There is also a predictable gender imbalance in the impact of this. Forty-nine per cent of women had lost pay or job promotions or had difficulty retaining jobs because of the need to care for sick children, compared to only 28 per cent of men. So the questions are, what sort of world are we creating as a result of global economic growth; what is the impact of this upon child growth and development; and what problems are we storing up for the near future by the patterns of family life that are emerging from this 'brave new world'?

Is this a matter of well-meaning academics scaremongering and bombarding us with statistics without sufficient analysis as to the real implications? Does it matter if children are no longer cared for so intensively within a traditional family structure? Do we fully understand the impact of these changing patterns of social life upon child development? Then, from within practical theology, what might the Christian tradition have to offer to this debate both ethically and indeed practically in terms of church-based work with families and children? This is the range of questions that will be explored further in the chapter.

The Importance of Early-Years Development

In order to address these questions I will focus upon some recent research which will contextualize this debate about the significance of working with children and families. I set this against a background where church-based work has, in the past at least, tended to concentrate upon school-age children, either through its direct involvement with church primary and secondary schools or with the traditional youth club or teenage activities. I suspect that although this continues in familiar forms, increasing numbers of faith communities are now offering facilities, either in terms of buildings or of groups, for work with pre-school children, particularly such activities as mothers and toddlers groups. So, for instance, a report from the UK's Northwest Development Agency on the contribution made by faith communities to civil society in the region (Northwest Development Agency 2003) records that of social activities offered for different age groups within the area, 26 per cent of these were for baby and toddler groups, twice the next highest category of activity and significantly higher than facilities for the elderly (8 per cent), which one might have expected would have been the greatest contribution.

Whilst one must be wary of reading too much into this, particularly as there is no comparative research available for previous years, it does suggest that working with this age group is now an important aspect of faith-based activity. There are a number of possible explanations. It could be a result of age structures within the northwest region, although that seems unlikely. It seems more likely that faith groups have done what has happened in terms of welfare activity over the years, that is, they have moved into a gap in the provision and begun to provide a service which has yet to be offered either by other voluntary organisations or by the statutory services. Note that this runs alongside recent increases in nursery provision and the general government policy to provide childcare so that mothers, in particular, can get back to work. This is offering something different – a facility for both mothers and toddlers. This may also reflect growing regulations about child protection, where it is easier to run groups where a parent remains and takes responsibility for their child or children, than to organize one where a child is left in the care of another adult.

It would appear that church-based and other faith group involvement with early-years activity is a pragmatic response to changing circumstances, offering a facility that has not yet been taken over by more formal provision. It is also possible that it reflects a growing awareness amongst mothers of the need for support and contact with other mothers at this vital stage of their, as well as the child's, development. Having run one such group myself, I am conscious that the main motivation, as publicly acknowledged by the local church, was to provide a support and social network for the mothers, as much as to assist in the development of the babies and toddlers.

I will argue, however, that this is only one possible justification for these activities, and that, as faith groups respond to the pressure placed on families by globalization, they need to recognize that this form of service is of even greater importance for the development of the children themselves. The implication is that church-based work with mothers and toddlers groups is in danger of becoming another zombie category, unless it becomes more aware of the other value of this work.

I draw upon the work of Dr Ross Thompson, a professor of psychology at Davis University in California, and his submission to the US Congress in February 2007 on the subject of the developing science of early childhood and early psychological development. The argument is that we now know much more about the importance of the early years for human development, both psychologically and neurologically. These two academic disciplines support the view that what happens in a child's life in the first few years is crucial for later stages of development. As Thompson suggests:

> Early relationships matter. Healthy development involves building strong minds, bodies and persons. The early years are a period of considerable opportunity for growth, and vulnerability to harm. Developing competence involves cognitive and non-cognitive capabilities. It is much better to prevent developmental problems from emerging than to try to remediate them later. (Thompson 2007: 2)

Whilst this might sound like a simple repeat of either common sense or homespun wisdom and experience, what is new is that there is scientific evidence to support the position. Brain development begins not at birth but pre-natally, once the nerve cells that will last a lifetime begin to be created. This begins the process of combining nature and nurture that shapes a person's life. How the brain becomes wired in the early years is the foundation for much that follows.

Developmental neuroscience suggests the following conclusions. Healthy brain development pre-natally is supported by good maternal nutrition, but can be undermined by maternal exposure to hazardous substances such as alcohol, environmental neurotoxins (e.g., lead-based paint) and controlled substances such as cocaine. So the damage to a child's brain can already have occurred by the time it is born. Once born, brain development spans one's entire life. Early childhood witnesses some of the most significant growth in the brain's developing architecture, including the 'blooming and pruning' of neural connections in different regions of the brain governing seeing and hearing, language and higher cognitive functions. These processes are substantially completed or well underway within the first five years of life. If these lower-level capacities are not effectively in place within that period, then it has implications for later stages of brain development. Advanced skills may be impaired by failures at the early stages.

This has obvious implications for educational development. The sort of experiences that will hopefully be encountered in the early years, such as letter-to-sound mapping, rhyming and listening to stories, provide the required base for further cognitive development, such as skills in literacy and numeracy. A child's curiosity, motivation to learn, self-confidence and capacity to relate to others are already being shaped at this stage. Current understandings of the structure of the brain suggest that cognitive and non-cognitive abilities cannot be identified with discrete areas, but that the brain is complex and highly integrated, so that capacities which do not develop at one level affect what happens at other levels. Cognitive and non-cognitive capacities are mutually influential.

One might feel that this degree of technical detail is of little importance for practical theology, but I would argue otherwise. The human capacity to develop relationships with others is surely central to the concerns of the Christian tradition, and, if these are being impaired by brain development in one's early years, then this has to be a matter for concern. There are also clear implications for how parents shape the lives of their offspring in these early years, and for how faith-based activity might best support and encourage appropriate development. Thompson notes that the evidence emerging from the USA is that young children are falling under the influence of negative experiences because of what is happening in the lives of their parents.

> Unfortunately, for many young children in the United States, experiences of chronic stress, neglect, or deprivation are major architects of their brain development, and help to account for some of the difficulties they face. This is because of how the brain responds neuro-biologically to stress. Chronic experiences of severe stress, especially in early life, can alter the functioning of brain-based stress systems – potentially causing the person to become hyper-responsive even to mild stressors – and can have important effects on physical health, immunological capacity and psychological well-being for this reason. (Thompson 2007: 5)

As Thompson suggests, children in socioeconomic hardship are especially vulnerable to such problems. As the brain's circuits consolidate over time, its actual plasticity and capacity to reshape decreases. Early years stress and trauma decreases the brain's ability to be adaptable and flexible and thus creates limits to a person's capacity to change.

What are the implications of this for parental relationships? Again the conclusions are not unexpected. 'Children grow and thrive in the context of close and dependable relationships that provide love and nurturance, security, responsive interaction, and encouragement for exploration' (Thompson 2007: 6). It is in the context of the family that the foundations are laid for further development, and if these are not there, problems are likely to arise later on. Security, stability, a space within which to experiment and yet still feel safe, with clear boundaries and continued love and support, are all obvious prerequisites for the development of both skills and confidence, just as much in a child's early years as in the school stages. In other words, what faith and church-based groups can offer to pre-school children is more than simply support to their mothers, although this too is clearly significant.

Early Years and Moral Development

What has been presented so far is only one piece of the jigsaw puzzle. The other crucial one is that of how recent research reveals that early years are also significant for an individual's moral development. Once again, it is Thompson's work which draws this out most clearly. Those familiar with theories of moral development will recognize that in the writing of scholars like Piaget and Kohlberg (both influential in the work of James Fowler and his writing on faith development which has been an influence upon church-based children's work), early years do not figure as being of any real importance. Young children are portrayed as externalized in their moral orientation, motivated to conform to external constraints by the fear of losing their parent's love or approval, and by the possibility of being rewarded in some way if they do as they are told. So they are presented as being pre-moral, or pre-conventional in Kohlberg's terms, not at a stage where they can begin to think and make judgements based on anything other than learned behaviour.

Whilst Thompson acknowledges that this dependence upon the parent–child relationship is indeed of importance, he also believes that such a view applied exclusively to early years development is now severely out-of-date. Why is this?

> Hardly any serious student of young children talks about their being egocentric, for example, because of the remarkable evidence that infants and toddlers are not only aware of differences in how people think and feel but are deeply interested in learning about others' mental states before their first birthday. (Thompson 2006: 2)

Thompson then uses this research to talk about the development of what we call conscience, defined as 'the cognitive, affective, relational, and other processes that influence how young children construct and act consistently with generalizable, internal standards of conduct' (2006: 2). Evidence of the development of conscience in young children includes: cooperation with a caregiver; unsupervised compliance with a standard; moral affect; moral reasoning; empathy with another and helping another (baby) in distress; an emerging 'moral self' as young children perceive themselves in ways relevant to moral compliance. Each of these has been studied in children under the age of six. The argument is that the beginnings of these moral developments are well underway by this stage, but that they tend to be ignored or underestimated by much of the literature, because it is only in later years that they reach fuller and more easily articulated development.

Amongst the factors that can contribute to early-years moral development are such things as social referencing – when an infant under 12 months old looks to the faces of adults for emotional clues as to their response to certain situations. The child can tell from the adult's facial expression or response, how a particular set of circumstances should be dealt with, and will learn to react and behave accordingly. This might include helping another child in distress, or showing sympathy for another. There is also evidence that three-year-olds can construct a distinction between what one wants to do, what one must do and what one does in compliance with another. Soon beyond this age, children are capable of recognizing the violation of behavioural conventions by other children, and of knowing that they are doing something wrong. Hence a degree of empathy and an emerging self-understanding are beginning to emerge in this preschool period.

What is being talked about here is not a fully formed conscience or sense of morality, but nevertheless the foundations or building blocks of these, mediated by key relationships, particularly with the parents, but also significant others in a child's life. If these relationships are impaired in any way, or if external pressures upon parents mean that the safe and secure space for child development is not available, then there are implications for moral development, as well as for the hard-wiring of the brain that is required for more straightforward cognitive skills. The research supports the argument that the relationship with the mother, in particular, is vital, and that if this is damaged or inadequate serious consequences may ensue. Early discussions between mother and child help the latter to establish a human connection between their own actions and the needs and welfare of others.

Much of this has been talked about before under the general heading of socialization: young children learn how to behave and how to relate to others by being part of a group of children, guided by an adult, but within a safe and secure environment. What Thompson is describing is more than this. Socialization can still be presented as essentially an external response or some form of learned behaviour, thus not based upon the internal development or what we might call conscience. I would go so far as to suggest that early-years development sees the beginning of that sense of connectedness with others in relationship that is central to all moral and indeed spiritual development. Remove the conditions in which this can become possible by destabilizing a young child's life, either through individual circumstances or possibly now because of global pressures, and the implications for the future are potentially immense. Likewise, if church or faith-based groups can create and support those conditions, then one has a significant and lasting opportunity to lay the foundations for further moral and spiritual development. In which case, activities such as mothers and toddlers groups are capable of offering more than just support networks for mothers, although that is clearly a vital component for this foundation-building. It also means that one needs to look critically both at the motivation and the practice of statutory or commercially based organizations which provide preschool childcare simply for economic reasons – that is, to allow mothers to return to the workforce as soon as possible. Where and how does the well-being and future (and indeed therefore) current development of the young child figure in the equation?

Embedding a specific quality of relationship is perhaps the criterion by which practical theology should be evaluating current activities, church-based and otherwise, when it comes to the care and upbringing of young children. What other evidence is available to support this view?

The Virus of Selfish Capitalism

Having reviewed some recent scientific evidence on the importance of working with young children and their families, the focus needs to shift towards the impact of global forces upon this area. I draw first of all upon the writing of Oliver James, a clinical child psychologist who has produced interesting research on the effects of what he calls the virus of selfish capitalism upon children and families. What does he mean by this term? He identifies four elements.

> The first is that the success of businesses is judged almost exclusively by their current share price. The second is a strong drive to privatise public utilities, such as water, gas and electricity… The third is that there should be as little regulation of business as possible, with taxation for the rich and very rich so limited that whether to contribute becomes almost a matter of choice. The fourth is the conviction that consumption and market forces can meet human needs of almost every kind. (James 2007: xiv)

As one might imagine, James sees the USA as the prime example of this virus, with Denmark being at the opposite extreme. His research has been global though, and he offers a number of personal stories and accounts to illustrate the argument. One of the contentious issues in the globalization debate is the extent to which the influence of the USA is predominant in Western cultures and beyond, and James is clear that this is indeed the case. He says that the most comprehensive study so far of globalization has been of 22 developing nations, and that this concluded that the more a nation is influenced by the USA, the more consumerist it becomes. It is particularly the elites of developing countries who are most likely to take on these characteristics and to display symptoms of having 'caught' the selfish-capitalism virus (James 2007: 34). Why should this be a problem in the quality of human relationships, and thus have an impact upon families and children?

As has been noted in earlier chapters, one of the most concerning trends resulting from this growing consumerism is the commodification of relationships. Success in this sort of commercial environment requires turning oneself into a marketable commodity and then promoting oneself on that basis. 'Career success depends largely on how well persons sell themselves, how nice a package they are, whether they are cheerful, sound, aggressive, reliable or ambitious' (James 2007: 10). Many corporations use psychological testing to identify the appropriate candidates for a post. Reality TV programmes trade off the capacity of celebrities to promote and project themselves as recognizable commodities. This is, however, damaging to relationships, as it runs the risk of reducing both oneself and others to objects to be manipulated and thus undermines true intimacy.

> In choosing friends or lovers you are swayed by their supposed value in the personality market, by looks or wealth or charisma, rather than by love. This leaves you feeling lonely and craving emotional contact, vulnerable to depression. There is always a feeling that you could have a 'better' partner or friend, or a fear that your value may fall, creating acute anxiety. (James 2007: 10)

What emerges is a particular form of narcissism, an unhealthy focus upon selected personal characteristics, those that are deemed to be currently 'marketable' both in the business world and in the sphere of individual relationships. The claimed antidote for the subsequent depression created by this virus is that one resorts to consumption in order to relieve the symptoms of a lack of authentic relationships. This is exactly what the global economy requires of course, a greater dependence upon purchasing the goods that might contribute to a better self image, or else forms of addiction that are supposed to compensate for real intimacy and commitment. Another familiar way of describing this is the difference between having and being, as suggested some years ago by Erich Fromm (1942). All of this has been exacerbated, according to James, by the four aspects of selfish capitalism now associated with a particular form of globalization.

It is interesting to note that James sees religion as a major antidote to the worst effects of the virus, even though he himself expresses no specific religious commitment. This is because religious people are likely to be less materialistic or to possess the virus goals and motivations, because they are more likely to be concerned with spiritual matters (James 2007: 14). Research amongst young people in the USA has supported this view, although even those believers who pursue self-seeking ends are prone to the virus, just like the rest of the population.

This is an important argument although one must be aware that James's book operates at a high level of generalization. This populist book is supported by detailed research which will be published in a more academic form, but his objective is to stimulate debate and to raise questions about the factors that currently damage human well-being. Our immediate concern is the ways in which he claims that the selfish capitalism virus harms the lives of children and families.

One of the more extreme and disturbing accounts of this impact comes from Singapore and the story of a young woman who is a successful merchant banker with two young children. An authoritarianism has clearly been at work in her relationships, and she now uses the same approach with her own children. This is by no means unusual in her culture, and one must beware of generalizing or of translating across cultures. James uses this example to illustrate a more general point about the controlling nature of many parent–child relationships. A controlling pattern is when parents use rewards, threats, deadlines and hectoring language, pressuring children to conform to their demands. Love is conditional upon the children falling into line with their parents' requirements. This is to be contrasted with a more supportive approach to child upbringing, which encourages greater autonomy and self-control.

At its most extreme, this coercive form of parenting leads to delinquency and moody offspring; even at a lower level it produces highly conventional and compliant children and young adults. James as child psychologist describes this as the child 'introjecting' the parent's values, or adopting them merely to conform and achieve a 'quiet life', rather than because the values are understood and shared. This type of behaviour later in life may be exactly the sort of conformist attitude that global capitalism also encourages and rewards. One does not 'rock the boat', or express personal views or judgements about what the organization requires, so the virus of selfish capitalism trades off this type of child rearing. The fear is that we are creating automatons who passively service the system, rather than thinking and questioning autonomous individuals, who contribute creatively to the greater human good. Another danger is that it results in a fragile self-esteem, too dependent upon external approval for personal validation and meaning. The fear of failure becomes a determining motivation and a possible source of mental paralysis. Many so-called 'high achievers' have experienced this form of parenting to some degree. As James says:

> Controlling parenting puts children at a high risk of both anxiety and depression. Depressed people can be divided into two main types. The 'dependent' kind are plagued by feelings of loneliness, helplessness and weakness; they chronically fear being abandoned and left uncared for by loved ones, and are desperate to be comforted, nurtured and protected. The other category of depressive is called 'self-critical' because they are afflicted by feelings of unworthiness, inferiority, failure and guilt. They are plagued by a fear of disapproval, criticism and lack of acceptance by others and are prone to harsh self-scrutiny. (James 2007: 166)

To the extent to which selfish capitalism encourages and breeds this approach to parenting, it is bound to have a detrimental impact upon parent–child relationships, and to further hamper the development of happy and well-balanced adults later in life. At least, that is the conclusion one feels obliged to reach, reading this particular text. I agree that there is a certain force behind this argument, and that one can recognize such tendencies both in oneself and others. One might also agree with the importance of the opposite approach of supportive parenting where the child learns to construct their own sense of meaning and values, but I do wonder whether James is in danger of idealizing parent–child relationships. However, there is more to his argument than this.

There are further worrying impacts of the virus upon both education, and the role and self-understanding of parents themselves. Education is becoming increasingly subject to commercial pressures, and the values which predominate in the business world are encroaching into this aspect of our existence. Learning is not seen as an end in itself, but as a means to the end of creating good producers and consumers (James 2007: 179). James refers to examples from the UK, where girls, in particular, appear to be under enormous pressure to succeed academically in order to construct themselves as marketable employees. Research has shown that this has led to a greater incidence of depression amongst this group. In two representative samples of 15-year-old girls, one taken in 1987 and the other in 1999, there was a rise in the percentage of depressed from the higher social class from 24 per cent to 38 per cent.

This is the period when girls began significantly to outperform boys in almost every academic subject and at every educational stage. However, the greater their academic success, the greater their emotional stress, according to this research.

> Something toxic had entered the social ecology, and this study identifies it as Virus-related. The main worries that were increasingly troubling the high-income girls were family problems, schoolwork, exams and their weight. Virus-infected children are more likely to come from disharmonious or broken homes. (James 2007: 180)

These pressures carry on into adult working life and it seems that women are likely to agree to long working hours and the demands that result from being ambitious at work. This is a particular concern in the UK where the number of people working more than 60 hours a week has more than doubled since 1998 (from 10 per cent to 26 per cent) and full-time British workers work on average 44 hours per week, which is the highest figure in the EU. What has happened to feminism one might ask, says James, and how have its initial ideals been appropriated by the success culture still operating according to the old models, but now driven even deeper into the culture by global capitalism? What is the impact of this upon families and children? James concludes:

> The truth is that in all the countries I visited, except Denmark, education is used mercilessly to put the needs of employers and economic growth ahead of those of children and emotional well-being. Just as the needs of parents have become paramount in most modern childcare manuals, with the damaging regimes dressed up as being for the child's good (leaving infants to cry themselves to sleep 'so they learn independence young', authoritarian discipline because 'they have to learn to obey the rules'), so with education. The education systems of the English-speaking countries, which purport to be giving children opportunities to become richer than their parents, are actively hostile to the flourishing of creativity and emotional development. (James 2007: 203)

How do parents themselves fare in this environment? Once again, James's conclusions are depressing. Despite all the advances made by women in recent generations, a 25-year-old woman today is three times more likely to suffer from depression than her counterpart of 50 years ago. The argument is that this very often stems from the devaluation of motherhood itself. Only paid employment is seen as a source of self esteem, and those who care for small children are looked down upon by those who have achieved their career ambitions, and are trapped in the cycle of mortgage repayments and other debts in order to finance a successful lifestyle. It may be that if more men were to become actively involved in caring for their children, it might reduce the damaging impacts of this, but this seems very unlikely to occur in the current economic climate. Parents under constant pressure to perform at work and to present the external trappings of affluence and success at home then create a less satisfactory environment for their children, and so the problems are intensified.

Of particular concern is the effect of this upon early-years development and, consistent with the other research already noted, James emphasizes that, for young children, the time between six months and three years, is highly formative in establishing patterns of relationships in later life. So if a woman returns to work during that period, then the least-worst substitute carer needs to be somebody who knows the child well and is also the sole carer. The evidence also suggests that group day care before the age of three is not advisable, and that one-to-one nannying is best. Deny appropriate care to children and one runs the risk that they will develop insecurity in their relationships and that they become overly aggressive and demanding of others. If mothers are aware of this evidence, yet still follow this route, they carry a burden of guilt despite their economic success. If they are not aware of it, then the problems will continue to multiply.

The background work on this was published in the 1960s and 1970s by John Bowlby, a doctor and psychotherapist who presented his ideas of attachment theory.

> According to Bowlby, the difference between secure and insecure is determined by the kind of care you received between the ages of 6 months and 3 years, and over 3000 empirical studies have broadly shown him to be correct. Emotional unresponsiveness or the physical absence of the carer at this age, or the combination of the two, create a state of fear that the carer will be emotionally unavailable. This anxiety endures into adulthood and is triggered by subsequent intimate attachments. (James 2007: 232)

The evidence on the impact of childcare is itself controversial and contested, and the arguments themselves are perhaps beyond the scope of this particular text. However, there is no doubt that there are risks involved in pursuing this route of responding to the needs of young children and one needs to ask exactly whose benefit is being served by this. Just how much is really economically driven, with the other arguments being tagged on later as a justification for mothers and fathers to pass the responsibility to early-years caring over to the paid professionals? This is dangerous territory for practical theology to stray into simply because most parents under pressure want to feel supported by the church in the decisions they take rather than being criticized and made to feel guilty. Does our work with young children collude with the economic objectives rather than challenging them by raising the serious questions of what the research actually reveals? If James is anywhere near correct then practical theology cannot divorce its concerns for families and children from political analysis and the impact of the global economy upon this aspect of our lives.

Global Inequality and Families

The previous section has concentrated upon the more affluent nations and ways in which globalization creates problems because of the affluence that has now been generated. Yet it is also clear that issues of inequality and lack of access to economic resources, either created or exacerbated by the forces of globalization, have a great impact upon many others. The overall question is that of the well-being of children and families, and therefore how practical theology might intervene in order to witness to its concern for these groups. Building upon the research already presented I will use a recent book by Richard Wilkinson, Professor of Social Epidemiology at the University of Nottingham, to argue that inequalities heightened by economic globalization are a further factor in damaging our care for young children (Wilkinson 2005).

He concludes that societies with more income inequality tend to be more severely affected by considerations of status and by issues of social rank. Social relationships begin to suffer, with evident lower levels of trust, increased levels of violence and higher levels of stress which impact upon well-being generally. Wilkinson is convinced that the central issue facing modern societies, thus affecting the health, happiness and quality of life of all, is that of the quality of social relations. Yet social relations are built upon material foundations, and inequalities of access to material resources have a direct effect upon our social relationships (Wilkinson 2005: 286). Societies face a stark choice between allowing 'might is right' to determine the distribution of its goods, and a more cooperative approach which is likely to yield a more even distribution, and to enhance the well-being of a higher proportion of its citizens. This is nothing new, but it is now played out in the context of global capitalism, where market forces are allowed to determine who gets what, and how.

How we are connected to one another in our economic life is determinative of how we connect to one another in our social and family lives:

> We are connected to each other through the self-interested opposition between buyers and sellers. Dependent upon our separate incomes, on what is in our bank account or wallet, to maintain respectability and avoid the shame of poverty we necessarily find other people's needs a threat to our own position and security. Because we feel we need to spend up to the maximum our incomes and credit ratings permit in order to keep up with escalating standards of decency, the cost of helping others financially involves a sacrifice of some of the material security needed to underpin our own social position. (Wilkinson 2005: 298–9)

Hence there is a conflict between the ways in which our personal and social relationships have been organized in the past and what the market model now requires of us. The combination of the market, emphasizing a narrow definition of self-interest, and inequality, tends to make us less social, reducing our willingness to cooperate and our concerns for each other's welfare. This is another way of interpreting the commodification of relationships already referred to. Once again there arises the question of what impact this is having upon children and families within the wider spectrum of social relationships.

Wilkinson argues that there are three major determinants of the health and well-being of the general population, those being low social status, weak social affiliations and emotional difficulties in early life. It is the last of these that is the main focus of this discussion. Recent research into factors affecting birth weight, have shown that mothers of low-birth-weight babies are more likely to have histories of stressful pregnancies. There is also a link between maternal stress and disease in later life involving levels of stress hormones such as cortisol. Maternal stress, however, does not just affect health in later life, but also leads to important behavioural differences. A study of almost 7,500 children found that maternal stress in pregnancy is a predictor of children's behaviour when they are three years old, with an increased incidence of the development of emotional problems.

> Research on the long-term health consequences of social and emotional development from birth into early childhood looks much like the biological side of what psychologists have been telling us for many years about the importance of early childhood. Poor attachment,

> domestic conflict, loss of a parent – all seem to have lasting effects on physical health. (Wilkinson 2005: 84)

Hence it can be seen that the research utilized by Wilkinson on physical health parallels the work done by Bowlby on the psychological impact of problems in the early years. This further reinforces concerns about the impact of globalization upon the relative economic status of families. What happens to children in their first three years of life sets the tone and patterns for their subsequent social relationships, very much as Thompson also argues from within a different scientific discipline. Wilkinson describes it like this:

> To fit any particular society, it is important to have the optimal balance in our social repertoire between affiliative behavioural strategies, on the one hand, and the timidity, fear and aggression appropriate to ranking systems, on the other. But rather than the balance being genetically fixed once and for all, the period of early sensitivity allows the hormonal influences on social behaviour to be adjusted in the light of early experience. We need to be biologically prepared for the particular character of social life. (Wilkinson 2005: 265–6)

The problem in modern societies in which children tend to grow up in a nuclear-family environment rather than as part of a wider social network as in earlier societies, is that the results of this early sensitivity can often look counter-productive. Many children are brought up amid great conflict and thus lack social skills, such as the ability to trust and cooperate, that are helpful in adult life. Others grow up in a secure and caring emotional environment, but that may ill-prepare them for the competitive and harsh world of global commerce. Thus there is a greater possibility of a disjunction between one's early experience and shaping for adult life, and the subsequent demands of the adult world. This itself leads to increased levels of stress and ill-being and further complicates the challenge of parenting which will follow. Combined with the higher levels of inequality, which are now an established part of the global economy, one can see that practical theology is justified in giving increased attention to biological, psychological and neurological research into the importance of human development in the early years. The challenge set by this is to decide how theology is to respond from within its own tradition, at a time when what have been the normative models for family life are themselves under threat. Are there positive strategies practical theology can present which reinforce the growing concern for early-years development and the role of parents often struggling in the context of a specific form of globalization?

The Family and the Christian Tradition

It has been shown how potential work with young children is of great significance for those of faith who offer support and resources to contemporary family life. Practical theology can now focus energy on this aspect of family work with confidence that it is more than simply a pragmatic response to a gap in secular provision. But this still leaves important questions about how one is to address wider concerns about family life within the context of a globalized economy and culture. Does the Christian tradition have insights and practical responses to offer despite the fact that one is dealing with a multi-faceted range of views on human relationships? I turn now to recent work by the American practical theologian, Don Browning (2007), who, along with others, has been engaged in a long-term project reviewing precisely this issue.

Pursuing a similar approach to this book, Browning proposes the view that any such project must involve a study of other disciplines which contribute ideas and research into human relationships. He also, however, suggests that what is now required is a worldwide revival and reconstruction of marriage, although he sees this is a long-term task and one that goes against the grain of some secular visions within the field. Nor is this simply a matter of emphasizing the need for jobs, for education and the economic liberation of women, which is the way that religious groups are sometimes prone to present the problems. But this is a reconstruction that Browning is calling for, so much more than an attempted return to the 'good old days' before global changes began to take effect. He terms this approach 'critical familism' and it will become clear what he means by this (Browning 2007: 247).

The starting point is an analysis and understanding of the ways in which modernity and globalization have changed the context for this area of human relationships. Unlike some other authors, he prefers to eschew the term postmodernity, and to focus upon modernity as it transforms itself under global influences. By modernity he understands the processes of technical rationality as expressed in both market capitalism and government bureaucracy. This covers all forms of political structure, including all versions of socialism, as well as market capitalism. Such forces are now being heightened by the spread of a special kind of globalization which is tending to encroach upon all countries whatever their culture and political heritage. In the terminology that I prefer to employ, globalization is rapidly becoming an enclosure and an all-consuming pattern of life, from which it is increasingly difficult to create and identify thresholds to other possibilities.

One set of ideas that lies behind this, and which has already been referred to in an earlier chapter, is that of the work of the German philosopher and social theorist Habermas when he talks about 'the colonisation of the lifeworld' (1984). What this means is that the values and steering mechanisms associated with the world of commerce and government increasingly impinge upon and then take over other areas of human life, such as the family or education, which have previously been directed by different and more personal values. So this is not just about global capitalism setting the agenda for personal relationships through commodification but also the ways in which bureaucratic rationality in the form of welfare policies and an expanded legal control impinge upon them. Yet, Browning argues, it would be a mistake to see these as simply taking over, because humans still possess the capacity to review such changes critically and to employ communications technology in an enlightened and thoughtful manner. So there may be thresholds after all, and ways in which a total dominance of global capitalist values can be resisted. One of these, he suggests, is through a reconstruction of the Christian understanding of marriage building upon the insights of other disciplines.

A source upon whom Browning draws is the American sociologist William Goode. In 1963 Goode wrote a major study of the ways in which relationships were then developing under the influence of modernization, showing how the extended family was on the wane and advocating instead what he called the 'conjugal' or 'companionate' family. At this point he believed that such new family patterns would bring greater happiness and freedom. Three decades later however, Goode has shifted his position somewhat as the evidence builds up that this particular reconstruction of family life is proving harmful to personal relationships, and is damaging intimacy in ways which we have already noted. The plurality of patterns of relationship, including higher numbers of divorces, more cohabitation and more births out of wedlock, seem to go hand in hand with growing poverty and declining well-being amongst significant percentages of women and children. A counter example would be Sweden, which has a stable high-divorce and family-disruption society, but relies upon a particular form of welfare support. Short of translating this system into other cultures and countries, Goode has no antidote to the problems that are building up elsewhere.

Browning then moves to the work of two other sociologists, David Popenoe and Alan Wolfe, who have studied the same social trends but come up with different solutions. Their statistics on marriage are themselves worthy of note.

> Since the 1960s, the divorce rate has more than doubled in the United Kingdom, the United States, France and Australia. During this same period, nonmarital births increased from 5% to 33% in the United States, from 4% to 31% in Canada, from 5% to 38% in the United Kingdom, and from 6% to 36% in France ... The marriage rate in all advanced countries has declined significantly. In the United States, there has been a 30% decline in the marriage rate since 1960, and overall there has been an 11% decline in the number of people over age 15 who are married. Much of this can be explained by later marriages and increased longevity. But some of this decline is due to increased lifelong singleness and cohabitation. (Browning 2007: 251)

Such trends have significant effects upon other areas of social policy. For instance, in the UK, the proposed explanation for the need for large numbers of new houses is the increased incidence of people living alone after marriage break-ups, particularly men. This raises a vital aspect of the reconfiguration of relationships, which is the number of absent fathers and the economic and behavioural impact of this upon young children and lone mothers. The classic 'liberal' response to all this in most Western societies is to accept these new patterns as the norm and then construct a welfare system that 'picks up the pieces' as best it can. The values that lie behind this, according to both Browning and Popenoe, are those of an expressive and utilitarian individualism – the type of 'what's in it for me' approach that discourages any notion of sacrifice or deeper long-term commitment to the institution of marriage. Whether this can in any way be reversed by government policies is itself a highly controversial issue. If Habermas is correct that the values of the systems world are as influential in all forms of bureaucratic control as they are in the spheres of commerce and business, then trying to use these to shape relationships will be counter-productive.

> Each of these forces disrupts the interactions of the 'lifeworld' and the intimate spheres of marriage and family. From the market comes the increasing absorption of both men and women into the wage economy and the subsequent erosion of time for parenthood and stable marital relationships. From state bureaucracy comes increased control of the education of our children, the rise of the welfare state, its pre-emption of family functions, the subtle transfer of dependencies from family to state, and the increased juridification of both formal and informal affectional relationships. (Browning 2007: 253)

Exactly what sort of solution might be proposed, assuming this interpretation is correct? Although the sociologists quoted by Browning reach similar conclusions about the need to reconstruct marriage as a social and personal institution, what none of them are prepared to acknowledge are ways in which religious groups and their values might play a significant role in this process. Browning argues that Christianity can be an important resource precisely through the critical familism mentioned earlier. In other words, such an approach does not advocate the family 'at any cost' and must acknowledge that there are circumstances where this form of relationship is not appropriate, but what it does do is to promote the ideal of the equal-regard, mother–father partnership where both parties have equal access to the responsibilities and privileges of both the public world of citizenship and employment and the domestic sphere of household maintenance and childcare.

It is important to understand what Browning means by 'equal regard'. His definition derives from the Christian principle of loving one's neighbour as oneself, but that valuing oneself is part of that overall equation:

> The 'other' must be loved equally to the self, but the self should be regarded equally to the other. This formulation of the meaning of Christian love is both faithful to the tradition, sensitive to the self-affirmations of women and minorities, and more adequate to the need of postmodern families for more flexibility between public and private realms. (Browning 2007: 127)

There is a further debate about the role of legal institutions within such a reconstruction. Will it suffice to try to change cultural patterns of relationship solely through religious values and practices, or is there a role also for the law to play a part in this process? Browning believes, from within an American context, that the two should cooperate, and thus stand a better chance of reconstructing marriage within society. How one responds to this suggestion will depend upon the nature of the relationship between church and state within a specific culture and raises issues that go beyond the scope of this chapter. It does seem to me, however, that Browning's proposal is worthy of serious consideration, and one way in which the Christian tradition can reinterpret its own teaching in a positive response to current problems within the sphere of intimate relationships.

The Question of Working Hours

Whilst this theoretical vision of how to reconfigure marriage is clearly of importance in the debate, it still leaves the question of how such a notion of equal regard might make a practical difference in the lives of families. A further dimension of Browning's work has been to offer a very specific proposal as regards the hours worked by two people within a marriage under current globally influenced circumstances. He offers a very simple suggestion that societies ought to develop a 60-hour working week for a husband and wife if they have children (Browning 2007: 284ff). Exactly how these hours are to be divided between a couple depends upon their individual circumstances. Although the idea is itself simple, Browning suggests that it both flows from a Christian perspective on relationships, and would have radical implications. Some Christians might view such a specific proposal as a distraction from more contentious issues, but Browning believes that something like this is necessary if the wider concerns about poverty and inequality are to be addressed. A considerable amount of research lies behind this idea and I will only touch upon this here.

The research found that a 60-hour working week allowed married partners enough time for outside activity, as well as to spend with each other. It also gave proper time and space for couples to spend with their children in ways that enabled intimacy and real relationships to develop. It also tended to create a balance between the working hours and respective satisfaction of both the man and woman, so, for instance, it might well mean that a mother would work part-time, and thus gain greater work satisfaction than either working full-time or not at all. Achieving that balance relates once again to Browning's notion of love as equal regard within the marriage relationship, so a theological motivation rests behind the proposal. The details of this suggestion would need careful working out, and the specific hours might vary according to different circumstances, but here at least is a concrete idea that could be debated and backed up by both empirical research and religious principles.

Reflexivity

Without pursuing Browning's ideas in greater depth, it is important to note that his general approach builds upon the understanding of the centrality of human communication as derived from, amongst others, Habermas. In short, the capacity of couples within a relationship to establish the agreement to share a 60-hour working week, for instance, depends upon openness, mutual respect and communication, that are themselves challenging and demanding. How a particular couple might reach such an agreement becomes a major cause for examination and research. The notions of reflexivity – a critical self-awareness and honesty – and the willingness to put this into operation within one's closest relationships become central to Browning's proposals. This begs certain questions about the human capacity to achieve reflexivity and the limits of this as determined by both external and internal factors. How many of us in reality move so far towards acknowledging that the other person exists in their own right and not as a means to our ends even in our closest and most intimate relationships? One might agree that this is the ideal of relationship, but then what are the constraints that pull us in the opposite direction of the strategic and instrumental relationships in which we act as if the 'other' existed for our benefit? Is Browning somewhat idealistic here in exactly the same way as James is? This question takes the discussion back to the debate about spirituality and models of the human being in the previous chapter and will emerge again in due course.

A final point that must be registered is that of understanding the economic and political context of decisions that governments make, and which influence directly the domestic and working lives of couples and thus, in due course, their children. It has been mentioned before that policies of getting women back into the labour market have a significant impact upon the provision of childcare and thus create a controversial debate about possible detrimental effects upon child development and behaviour. In the UK at least, there has been an explicitly political motivation behind this since 1997 when New Labour took office. One of its prime objectives was to avoid raising levels of direct taxation as this, at the time, made any political party unelectable. Yet it was clearly part of its agenda to increase spending on public services so other means had to be found of raising government revenues in order to achieve this. The obvious solution was – and perhaps still is – to get as many people as possible into work so that more people were paying income tax and less were eligible for benefits. This meant getting more women into work and the consequent requirement to provide higher levels of childcare and nursery provision. I suggest that this political motivation took priority over concerns about the possible impact of this policy upon young children. This takes place within the wider setting of the impact of the global economy upon the financial health and stability of the country and the arguments presented about the need to be competitive. This is not to say though that this is the only policy impacting upon family life, nor that other policies might not work in the other direction – for instance the number of hours that it is possible for part-time workers to operate before benefits start to suffer. That again is probably a politically motivated decision.

What this highlights is the impact of responses to global economic forces upon decisions that have a significant influence upon the quality of family life. The boundaries between politics, economics, social and cultural values are inevitably blurred and it is only within that complexity that religious insights and critiques can play a role in the debate. This chapter has shown how practical theology must take notice of the research emerging from other disciplines if it is to make a convincing and effective contribution to the discussions about children and family life, and has offered at least some suggestions as to how this might progress.

Chapter 7

Work and the New Economy

Introduction

The previous chapter raised the issue of the length of working hours and the impact that this might have upon family life. In this chapter the focus shifts onto the subject of work itself and ways in which globalization, or, at least a particular form of it, is now affecting working patterns, creativity and what is known as work–life balance. Why should this be of concern to practical theology? Apart from the obvious point that theology should be concerned with the whole person and therefore with all aspects of life, including employment, it is clear that there are significant personal ramifications of the ways in which working practices are changing. How much time and energy do people have left to devote to their personal and family lives? When that has been accounted for is there anything left to give to voluntary activity such as commitment to a local faith group or community? One of the most familiar complaints from clergy and others who run voluntary groups is that people no longer have the spare time to give to such activity. To what extent this is an excuse or whether it really is as a result of greater demands made by the global employment market is a matter of debate, but the end result is that the levels of social capital supposedly available appear to be diminishing. This is obviously connected to some of the arguments addressed earlier about decreasing attachments to place and the current complexities of personal identity.

Another aspect of this might be Christian involvement in work place ministry as it has been developed by the Industrial Mission movement. This has traditionally been understood as an attempt to make contact with people outside church boundaries, but also as the church's means of engaging more effectively with economic and social life. Although in the current era of cutbacks and the growing marginalization of sector ministry, as the emphasis shifts towards mission interpreted as 'fresh expressions of church', such chaplaincy models fall out of favour, one might argue that Industrial Mission has always been a 'fresh expression'. Certainly one can surely justify a deep and continuing Christian involvement with issues of work and employment both pastorally and in terms of social justice. It is with these in mind that this chapter carries the debate forward through an engagement with the forces of globalization.

Rather than attempting to survey the full range of what work now involves, I am going to concentrate upon one specific profession, that of engineering, in order to illustrate the general issues that are emerging. The argument will show how this well-established and formerly reasonably high-status profession is being undermined by the changes associated with globalization in the workings of what is called 'the new economy'. Following this there will be an examination of the more general concerns about work–life balance and why this is important for practical theology.

The Engineering Profession

In July 2006 the UK press reported the following story. James Dyson, famous for designing the domestic appliance known world-wide as the 'Dyson' (a type of bagless vacuum cleaner), in despair at the way in which UK schools were neglecting budding young engineers, was proposing to set up a new academy of design and enterprise. The report went on to say that this was just the latest example of the drastic steps that business leaders were forced to take in order to arrest the decline in skills and competitiveness. The major fear is that China and India are about to race ahead leaving economies such as the UK far behind. Figures quoted suggest that the UK produces 24,000 engineering graduates a year, compared with 300,000 in China and 450,000 in India. Questions are raised about the government's real commitment to engineering and science in its educational policies despite its claims to be placing an increased emphasis upon these areas of the curriculum.

As well as formulating a new course on business and engineering, the academy would offer courses on Mandarin. Mr Dyson himself is quoted as saying: 'The school will allow young people to explore ideas, experiment and solve real world problems. We want to encourage future generations of design engineers'. Support will also be forthcoming from the aerospace groups Rolls Royce and Airbus and the Formula One teams of Williams and MacLaren. However, it was also noted that the company had moved its manufacturing plant to Malaysia four years previously, thus cutting 800 jobs, but that it retained a team of engineers and designers at its UK headquarters. This latest scheme is in addition to Rolls Royce's two-year project to find the most original science teachers in the country and the recent concerns about the long-term future of the aerospace industry which, along with the automotive industry, is probably the largest manufacturing sector remaining in the UK.

Within this brief account it is possible to identify ways in which globalization is now impacting upon the engineering profession. Yet one must be cautious in simply attributing all determining factors to one cause or set of related causes. What I aim to present are ways in which globalization creates both enclosures and thresholds for the engineering profession. Enclosures are areas where people feel trapped or constrained by developments beyond their control and thresholds are the possibilities that are glimpsed of new and exciting developments, often despite of or in the midst of the enclosures. I hope in this way to guard against any form of determinism, the suggestion that 'things are bound to be this way', which invariably leads to pessimism or a fatalistic attitude towards the future.

Issues Raised by Globalization

For the moment it will be useful to identify the range of issues which arise from the Dyson story. First is that of global competition and, in particular, the rise of China and India and indeed other Far Eastern economies. This is the current background to wider concerns about the impact of globalization upon the developed economies. It includes worries about the loss of manufacturing jobs and the apparent gap in skills and education between different parts of the world. Is this inevitable or can something be done about it? We will see shortly that attempts are being made to tackle the educational dimension of this but that hopes of translating this into large-scale changes in the numbers involved in manufacturing itself are less evident. Second is the role of design and innovation within the engineering profession. Even though manufacturing may inevitably be shifting to the Far East because of lower labour costs, is it still possible that creative and innovative research and design functions can be retained in the developed nations? The hope clearly is that this will be the case. Yet this raises a further set of issues. What sort of companies or businesses will be able to survive and flourish in this context? Will these be the larger and transnational corporations operating to the rules of the global economy, themselves determined, as we shall see, by employment practices that may or may not be conducive to creative engineering? Companies that are profit and shareholder driven bring their own constraints and limitations for many who are concerned about more than simply earning their living and also raise wider ethical and economic questions. Perhaps alongside this will run the capacity of smaller and networked businesses to provide spaces and opportunities for greater freedom to think creatively and critically within the profession. Does big business equal enclosure and small business equal threshold, or are both in fact locked into the same system?

What is the role of government in all of this? It would appear that any government's major concern is about remaining competitive in the global economy. Hence issues about the quality and quantity of the teaching of science and engineering, both at school and graduate level, are simply geared to internal economic measures and have no wider vision of the role of the professions let alone an understanding that these are spheres where exciting and significant breakthroughs occur that are of more than financial benefit.

One might be tempted to ask where human beings as human beings come into this picture, if at all. Is inspiration and inducement into engineering really going to emerge from within such an economically determined context? Why would anybody even think about becoming an engineer? Is it for the money or in spite of the money, or perhaps for some other set of motives? Where is the evidence for this and whose interests are being served when governments insist on playing a leading role in addressing the issues?

The Rise of the New Economy

I will now examine the argument that the current context is the result of a series of decisions and policies that some within the field of politics and sociology term the rise of the new economy. In other words, there are clear and identifiable changes within the global economic structure that derive directly from deliberately pursued political decisions and that reflect the interests of a certain set of key players. One of the major contributors to this theory is the sociologist Castells who has written one of the seminal works in recent years on the subject of what he calls the Network Society (Castells 2001).

This new economy has emerged during the last quarter of the twentieth century and is characterized by three distinctive features. First it is informational in that the productivity and competitiveness of all agents in the economy (firms, regions or nations) depend upon their capacity to generate, process and apply knowledge-based information. Secondly, it is global as the core activities of production and consumption, as well as their components (capital, labour, technology, markets, etc.), are organized on a global scale. Finally it is networked because it is through networks that competition is played out on the global stage. The information technology revolution has been instrumental in creating this new set of conditions and both the constraints and possibilities that flow from them (Castells 2001: 77). What are the implications of this for the ways in which work is now organized?

Castells suggests that companies operating in this new environment have a number of strategies that they can pursue towards both skilled and unskilled labour (2001: 254). These are:

- Downsize the firm, keeping the indispensable highly skilled labour force in the north while importing inputs from low cost areas (very much the Dyson approach).
- Subcontract part of the work to their transnational establishments and to auxiliary networks whose production can still be internalized through the network enterprise system.
- Use temporary labour, part-time workers or informal firms as suppliers in the home country.
- Automate or relocate tasks for which the standard labour-market prices are too high.
- Obtain from the labour force agreement to more stringent conditions of work and pay as a condition for the continuation of their jobs, thus reversing social contracts established under more favourable conditions for labour.

It is possible that any combination of these will be encountered in specific situations, depending upon local conditions and decisions. The effect is to draw all countries into this system and to create a convergence of labour-market conditions across the globe. Furthermore, as Castells says: 'The pressure towards greater flexibility of the labour market and toward the reversal of the Welfare State in Western Europe come less from the pressures derived from East Asia than from the comparison with the United States' (2001: 254). Any company wishing to compete on equal terms with a US based business will have little choice but to follow the same route of creating greater labour flexibility. Hence 'lean production, downsizing, restructuring, consolidation, and flexible management practices are induced and made possible by the intertwined impact of economic globalization and diffusion of information technologies' (Castells 2001: 255). So although there is not a unified global labour market, similar patterns of labour organization emerge across national boundaries. Was this inevitable though? Castells suggests not:

> This model is not the inevitable consequence of the informational paradigm but the result of an economic and political choice made by governments and companies selecting the 'low road' in the process of the transition to the new, informational economy, mainly using productivity increases for short-term profitability. These policies contrast sharply, in fact,

> with the possibilities of work enhancement and sustained, high productivity opened up by the transformation of the work process under the informational paradigm. (Castells 2001: 255)

What begins to emerge from this, assuming Castells is correct, is that the way that engineering is now being shaped as a result of the forces of globalization is only one possibility, albeit the one that leads to short-term gain for some but at the expense of others. Is this good for engineering or good for engineers? If one contrasts what is occurring with other possibilities then one might argue that it is not. What we do have at the moment is a loss of jobs in the developed world combined with more stringent working conditions and the general demise of earlier victories gained by the labour movements. Increasing instability and job insecurity are combined with the downgrading of newly incorporated urban labour in industrializing countries. This is not the result of the structural logic of the informational economy, which could just as easily have led to higher levels of secure employment and greater opportunities for investment and innovation. Instead, the use of networking and the political decision to create a more mobile and volatile labour market have undermined such possibilities. Now these processes are 'locked in' it is going to be extremely difficult to reverse them.

Agencies such as the International Monetary Fund, and national government organizations have suggested that the problems of rising unemployment, income inequality and social polarization are the result of a skills mismatch, exacerbated by a lack of flexibility in the labour market. So there is a shortage of requisite skills to enable people to take advantage of the new economy and this is to be tackled through the educational system. However, some now argue that the evidence for this is actually extremely thin and that simply increasing the number of people in training will not itself create jobs that have now gone overseas. Castells documents the evidence for what has been happening in the USA in terms of unemployment and growing inequality (2001: 298), but also points out that similar trends are visible elsewhere in the developed world. The new vulnerability of labour is not confined to low-skilled jobs but is spreading up the labour-market hierarchy and into the ranks of professionals. Political parties of all persuasions on both sides of the Atlantic are pursing the same policies with very much the same results.

> Membership of corporations, or even countries, ceased to have its privileges because stepped-up global competition kept redesigning the variable geometry of work and markets. Never was labour more central to the process of value making. But never were the workers (regardless of their skills) more vulnerable to the organization, since they had become lean individuals, farmed out in a flexible network whose whereabouts were unknown to the network itself. (Castells 2001: 302)

This is the wider context in which engineering is now operating, one in which instability and uncertainty have been deliberately built into the system in ways which discourage individuals from challenging the decisions and policies of their employers, and which may also act as a disincentive for businesses themselves to invest in innovative or high-risk projects. Unless a project can show a swift profit turn-around for its investors – within 12 months is the figure mentioned in some companies, where the realistic lead time for research and development would be expected to be considerably longer – then there is no chance of funding. The more 'competitive' the global economy becomes, the less likely it is that smaller companies will survive or that general deteriorating working conditions will be reversed.

Work in the New Economy

The picture that is emerging is increasingly pessimistic, and points to the possibility that engineering, along with many other spheres of employment, finds itself engulfed by economic forces that threaten to stifle creativity and innovation within the profession. Stringent working conditions, and lack of long-term investment by companies not prepared to buck the trend of simply acquiescing to the demands of shareholders, suggest that it is going to become more difficult to recruit people who are interested in anything other than earning a living. Ideas of vision, of serving the wider public, or that engineering as a profession carries a sense of vocation, seem to be losing ground. Enclosures rather than thresholds are predominant in this new economy.

Before we move on to examine the detailed arguments about globalization, and then to ask where and how alternatives to the current system begin to appear, we need to press more deeply into this hostile territory in order to complete the negative side of the picture. This takes us into ideas about the nature of work itself and the writings of an American sociologist, Richard Sennett. In his most recent book, *The Culture of the New Capitalism* (2006) he offers an interpretation of working life as it is developing within the largest US and global companies. By this he means businesses with at least 9,000 employees. He is clear that what he is saying about these is not yet true of many smaller companies, but that these are the path breakers and trend setters of the new capitalism whose means of operating will influence others or prove to be the pattern of the future. They may be the tip of the iceberg at the moment, but more companies will soon be falling into line.

The days when companies were organized along military lines where everybody knew where they fitted into the structure, but where there was also a degree of security, stability and loyalty on both sides, are receding fast. What lies behind this? The shift from managerial to shareholder power is central. Sennett identifies the breakdown of the Bretton Woods agreements during the 1970s as the point when the shift became possible (Sennett 2006: 38). This enabled wealth to move more freely around the globe and for rich nations and significant investors such as giant pension funds to search out potentially profitable businesses as a source of swift profit. Once this began to happen, a new driving force came into play, one which had no real interest in or concern for the culture of an individual company, or even for the nature of the business. Only share value motivated the investment. This has been called 'impatient capital'.

The time scales involved in the investment market now began to shorten dramatically. Whereas in 1965 American pension funds held stock on average for 46 months, by 2000 this figure had fallen to 3.8 months. Companies came under pressure to present themselves in their best possible light to potential shareholders in this 'beauty parade' in order to attract investment. This often meant appearing to be dynamic and flexible rather than stable and secure. Higher staff turnover and the willingness to rationalize by cutting overhead costs by shedding staff, became the signals that a business had moved into this category, whether or not such actions were really in the best longer-term interests of the company.

Alongside this has run a propensity to centralize management structures and focus control at higher levels in the company. This has been aided by the implementation of more sophisticated information technology and the possibility of replacing lower-level staff with automation. Why employ people when machines can do the job faster and more cheaply? As Sennett reminds us, only the larger businesses with the resources to invest are initially able to go down this route, but they are the ones which are held up as the gateway to a more profitable future.

What are the consequences of this for the nature of work itself? We have seen some of these in Castells's comments about the increase of part-time work and shorter working contracts. High mobility and flexibility become paramount. Temporary work currently accounts for 8 per cent of the workforce in the USA (Sennett 2006: 49). But this is only one facet of the restructuring that now characterizes such companies. Greater degrees of uncertainty, inbuilt instability and shorter-term projects and agreements become the norm for staff in this environment. What are the true costs of this approach? Sennett suggests that although the financial rewards appear to be significant, what now happens is that there is a decrease of loyalty to the business, a loss of informal trust (social capital) between the staff, and indeed a weakening of the institutional knowledge that often characterizes more stable businesses. People's willingness to 'go the extra mile' on behalf of the business in return for feeling that one's work is valued and appropriately rewarded is eroded. As in the earlier days of capitalism a worker becomes a 'cog in the machine', of purely instrumental value, serving the end of increasing shareholder value rather than the internal nature of the work itself.

This may have a direct impact upon the well being of the employees.

> Pressure becomes a self-contained, deadening experience in firms with low social capital, and employees who experience pressure on these terms are far more likely to become alcoholic, to divorce, or to exhibit poor health than people working more than ten hours daily in high-loyalty firms. (Sennett 2006: 66)

This in turn begins to impact upon the nature of the work itself, especially when this has traditionally depended upon longer time scales for its research and development functions. Placing strict limits upon the time scale within which projects have to yield a return on the investment will inevitably begin to restrict the type of project that wins funding. Either that or they will learn to 'play the game' and to present projects in ways that appear to minimize the time commitment, and then hope that having once won the funding they will be able to stretch the time out if not the funding. Integrity rapidly becomes another victim of this type of pressure. Delayed gratification as a motivating factor is abandoned both for the investors and the workforce and this has an impact upon levels of commitment to the business. Unless rapid or immediate results can be shown, then nobody is allowed to gain from the work itself. This also means that the wider social networks and relationships which are often important within a research-based business are put under threat simply because groups are forced into competing between themselves as a means of obtaining the cheapest product and forcing down labour costs.

Sennett also suggests that this heralds the spectre of uselessness for many employees. How long will my role in the company last, and what happens to me when I am no longer profitable or useful? Older employees more accustomed to having a secure position within the structures, and therefore also more confident at challenging and questioning, become a liability and tend to be replaced by younger people who now accept that 'nothing lasts for ever' and that there are no 'jobs for life' any longer. They are prepared to keep their heads down and to get on with the task for as long as it happens to last, and then to move on.

What is also in danger of being lost is what Sennett calls craftsmanship. By this he means the understanding that one can derive satisfaction from being able to commit oneself thoroughly to a particular task or function and devote time and energy to it over the longer term. Pride in one's work and pleasure from having done a good job no longer count for much in this new mobile and flexible environment. The skills and experience that have often been built up over a long period of time become a liability rather than an asset, as the prime directive is the willingness to abandon what one has been doing and move seamlessly into another sphere of work, whether or not one has the aptitude or commitment to do it justice. Skimming across the surface and giving the impression of being in command of the latest task become more important than a willingness to 'dwell' and give real consideration to a project. Everything is 'for the time being only' as Bauman puts it (2006: 116–18). This must have its human and business costs for those who need to give real time and attention to their work, and one assumes that this applies to the more innovative and creative aspects of engineering. This presents a pessimistic scenario for the future of the profession, particularly as larger companies come to dominate the field in the face of global competition.

Who runs Globalization? China or the USA?

Who is controlling the processes of economic globalization? Turning first to the engineering profession itself, one can rapidly see that China is starting to challenge the former dominance of the USA. One major US company, GE plastics, is now well on the way to selling $1 billion's worth of advanced materials in China over the next two years (Fishman 2005: 216). Manufacturing is booming, and there is a clamour for places in higher education from budding engineers and scientists. GE has already opened a giant industrial research centre in Shanghai, and in 2006 expected to employ 1,200 people in its Chinese laboratories. It has also set up scholarships at leading Chinese technical universities.

This type of expansionary programme is getting internal support from the Chinese government. The country already has 17 million university and advanced vocational students (up more than threefold within 5 years), the majority of whom are in science and engineering. They quote a figure of 325,000 engineers being produced in 2005, which is five times the number in the USA where the number of engineering graduates has been declining since the early 1980s. Even more worrying, 40 per cent of students who enter the engineering track at US universities change their mind. Even so, the current gap between the USA and China in terms of research resources remains substantial. So, for instance, the US government authorized $3.7 billion to finance research into nanotechnology in 2004 and China simply does not have the funding or the infrastructure to support programmes on this scale.

However, the gap is beginning to narrow. In more mainstream applied technology and innovation, China spent $60 billion on research in 2004. The only countries spending more were the USA and Japan, with figures of $282 billion and $104 billion respectively. The USA still has twice as many researchers as China (1.3 million compared to 743,000), but this figure is clearly set to move in favour of China over the coming years. As we have seen from earlier examples, the pattern might well be that production is shifted east for obvious reasons, but that more sophisticated research facilities remain in the USA and Europe. How long will this last as China speeds further down the road of industrial development?

Another Chinese example comes from the city of Chengdu, capital of Sichuan province in southwest China. This covers an area slightly larger than California but is three times as populous (Fishman 2005: 218). There are about 107 million people in the province, 43 universities and 1.2 million scientists and engineers. At the moment its fragmented transportation system prevents it from rivalling cities further east as a manufacturing centre, but it is promoting its plentiful, relatively low-cost, intellectual expertise through its new research corridor, the West High-Tech Zone. Motorola has built its newest research centre in the province, and regards this as a world centre for software engineering. Other major enterprises such as Intel, Ericsson, Siemens, Alcatel and Fuji Heavy Industries of Japan already have bases within the province. This is part of a wider picture in which between 200 and 400 foreign companies have established research centres in China since 1990. This is not just about tax incentives and lower labour costs, but is also related to the growing consumer base in the country. As Fishman says though, the probable outcome of this continued growth (China's aim is a year-on-year growth of 8 per cent in its GDP, and this is being achieved), is a saturation of the markets and concerning levels of overcapacity. While China catches up and other developed nations stand still or decline, questions of economic and political conflict will come to the fore. Is this level of growth sustainable, and what are the costs both for China itself, let alone the rest of the world? How far will the USA allow this process to progress before it flexes its muscles in order to protect its own market share and economic dominance?

The figures of the loss of jobs from the USA to China are difficult to assess as the US government does not collate them, but one study in 2004 showed that during the course of three months, 58 US companies, 55 European companies and 33 from other Asian countries, all announced plans to move jobs to China (Fishman 2005: 273). This was a marked increase for the USA, where in 2001 only 25 companies announced shifts to China. The study concludes that US companies moved 400,000 jobs to other countries over the course of 2004, twice the number that had gone three years before. Another significant change is the nature of the posts that have gone to China. Whereas they used to be in the fields of electronics and toys, now they are across a broader section of the employment pool. This is all part of the growing drive for labour flexibility that is central to the new economy. Local labour forces will have less bargaining power as the threat is always present that jobs will simply be moved to other (cheaper) countries if terms favourable to management are not accepted.

Another implication of these changes is the possibility that companies who retain research facilities in the USA and Europe will find that they reach the point where they no longer have the critical mass of people to remain innovative and competitive. Where will the global entrepreneurs and innovators be located in years to come? As Fishman says:

> One of China's most potent economic weapons is its ability to attract entire industry clusters, acquiring the critical masses of companies that catalyze the creative ferment that leads to rapid innovation. Global telecommunications and regular air links may go a long way to closing the distances for Cox's American army of global entrepreneurs, but Americans stringing together opportunities in distant lands will have to spend a lot of time re-creating the network of relationships that has been lost as America's industrial clusters depopulate, devolve, or both. (Fishman 2005: 276)

So who exactly will be in control of the process of economic globalization in a few years' time, and what might be the implications for engineers and indeed scientific research if the balance of power shifts decisively to the east as seems likely? It is possible of course that these arguments are being exaggerated. It may be that China and India are experiencing their own industrial revolutions, and simply playing catch up with the West, and that matters will even themselves out over time. It may also be the case that such rapid rates of growth are not sustainable, and that internal political factors will start to drag China back as instability and uncertainty sets in, as it already has elsewhere. However, when one considers that China and India between them possess a third of the world's population, it is clear that their economic expansion still has a long way to go, and must have a dramatic impact upon the rest of the world, if it continues along the current path. Although the USA still dominates the global economy, this picture is changing.

Large or Small? Short-Term or Long-Term?

We have already touched upon the question of the scale of enterprise that is most likely to survive and thrive within the new economy, but it does need to be emphasized that there are significant questions about who is going to benefit from economic globalization in its current form, and that practical theology needs to be alert to these issues. So here is an example from Canada that sends out warning signals (Bauman 2006: 71).

This story was reported in a regular column called *Countryside Commentary* in the newspaper *Corner Post* on 24 May 2002 in an article written by the strategic policy advisor to the Christian Farmers Federation of Ontario. The article was entitled 'The collateral damage from Globalization'. The author reported that each year more food is produced, but fewer people are employed in the process, because there is a more prudent use of resources. So in the four years up to February 2002, 35,000 workers disappeared from Ontario's farming statistics, made redundant by technological progress and replaced by new and labour-saving technology. However, whilst one would have anticipated that the subsequent increases in productivity should have made rural Ontario richer and farmers' profits would have soared, there has been no sign of this. The conclusion can only be that the profits have accrued elsewhere in the system.

The apparent explanation for this is globalization, to the extent that it has spawned a series of mergers and buyouts by the firms that supply farm produce. This is justified by the argument about remaining globally competitive through creating larger and possibly monopolistic groupings of companies. It is these businesses that then reap the benefit of higher productivity. The article concludes:

> Large corporations become predatory giants and then capture markets. They can – and do – use economic power to get what they want from the countryside. Voluntary exchanges, trading goods between equals, are giving way to a command-and-control countryside economy.

Again, one needs to be wary of such comments, as they are clearly written from the perspective of the local farming community and represent a particular vested interest. Yet they are consistent with what is evident within other sectors of US and European economies. What is happening is that globalization is being used as a reason for concentrating power within fewer businesses on the grounds that this is the only way to remain competitive given the growth of China and India. Only the larger companies who have economies of scale will be able to survive and compete. The alternative to this is a growth in smaller and more niche-marketed or specialized companies who rely more on networks and IT than on substantial plants or workforces. Volume production in most industries has moved east.

One needs to question whether this movement is inevitable, or whether the argument is sometimes presented as a justification for decisions that are really being made for other reasons. Who gains from these decisions and who loses out? Is the predominant strategy that of chasing short-term profit, whatever the longer-term local costs? It is easier for companies to transfer production to the other side of the world than for the workforce, with its local commitments, to even consider such a move. But the whole argument rests on the assumption that 'in the highly competitive global economy big is beautiful once again'. One wonders on what grounds such a view can be supported and justified.

Yet if 'large versus small' is a dimension of the current debate about globalization, then there is clearly also a direct link to questions of time scale and subsequent concerns about stability and security for projects and employees. The new economy demands flexibility and the capacity to shift from one set of skills to another at almost a moment's notice, whatever the personal costs. Bauman presents a powerful analogy. He likens this process to the contrast between bullets fired from a ballistic weapon and the new smart missiles. The trajectory and direction of the bullet is predetermined, making it an ideal weapon in positional warfare where targets remain static and predictable. However, once targets become more volatile and unpredictable in their movements, bullets become ineffective and smart missiles that can themselves change course and track the target are what is required.

> Such smart missiles cannot suspend the gathering and processing of information as it travels, let alone finish them – its target never stops moving and changing direction and speed, so that plotting the place of encounter needs to be constantly updated and corrected. (Bauman 2006: 117)

This is a way of describing the 'instrumental rationality' that appears to dominate current business culture. In other words, it is no longer simple to calculate the ends for which a particular weapon is the means of destruction. The target itself may change en route, and the missiles will be programmed to choose the target once they are in flight. So some sort of general capacity to adapt and then pursue a goal that might change as one moves is of more value than the old ability to pursue a pre-identified and predetermined goal. The missile must learn as it goes along, and what matters is the ability to learn fast, forgetting what must now be abandoned and ignoring what might have claimed to be important information when the journey began. So knowledge itself becomes disposable: useful 'for the time being only' and to be disposed of as soon as the target changes.

This has considerable implications for teaching and training, which used to be based on the assumption that imparting certain skills and knowledge was required in order to equip people for predictable and identifiable tasks. If this has now changed – and one can recognize enough of Bauman's descriptions of 'liquid life' to see how this might be the case – then it will have an effect upon how people have to be prepared for their working lives, even within the fields of engineering and scientific research. It will not do any longer to train people to follow a specific career path or a sub-discipline within a profession, because that will leave them 'high and dry' when the task changes and the target has shifted. It is the more general capacity to let go of what appeared to be important in order to adopt what is now important that is required. The question though, is that of the depth of knowledge and understanding that will be acquired once this more superficial approach begins to take over. Is it a matter of knowing a little about everything, or just enough to bluff one's way through the labyrinth, rather than of accumulating the knowledge which comes from time-bound experience within a particular field? If teaching and training themselves become so geared to these requirements of the new economy what standards will remain? Is such short-termism really of benefit to skills acquisition and building up a high-quality work force with an appropriate depth of knowledge? Globalization used as a justification for both large-scale production and research facilities dominated by global companies and then smaller and smaller time-scale approaches to skills and working practices needs to be questioned.

Nation States or Global Business?

Who is 'running the show' and who benefits from globalization? The exact balance between the power of nation states and that of companies is a matter for continuing debate, but it is worth at this stage looking at how companies operate in the new economy. Is it owners, senior managers (CEOs) or shareholders who determine what is to happen? According to the French sociologist Pierre Bourdieu, it is none of these.

> It is in fact, the managers of the big institutions, the pension funds, the big insurance companies, and, particularly in the United States, the money market funds or mutual funds who today dominate the field of financial capital, within which financial capital is both stake and weapon. These managers possess a formidable capacity to pressure both firms and states. (Bourdieu 2003: 28)

Their bargaining strength means that they can effectively impose upon others what is termed a 'minimum guaranteed shareholder income'. Thus ever higher profits become the immediate and short-term goal of any business, and are often achieved through downsizing and labour reductions. Bourdieu is close to suggesting that this is some sort of infernal machine that operates according to its own internal logic, and almost behind the backs of the people apparently running the system. Stock market value becomes the only measure of success, and, if values fall, the system demands it own victims or sacrificial lambs.

> Thus has come into being an economic regime that is inseparable from a political regime, a mode of production that entails a mode of domination based on the institution of insecurity, domination through precariousness: a deregulated financial market fosters a deregulated labour market and thereby the casualization of labour that cows workers into submission. (Bourdieu 2003: 29)

The new economy is dominated by individuals who are international rather than belonging to any particular state, who are polyglot and poly-cultural. It is immaterial and 'weightless' in that it circulates information and cultural products rather than consumer durables. In other words it belongs to a cultural elite who appear to form an 'economy of intelligence'. By contrast, those who fail to benefit from the advances that are being made, are somehow lacking in the required skills and intelligence to work out how to play this new system. This is a new form of the survival of the fittest. So it not straightforwardly the case that companies themselves are the immediate and obvious beneficiaries of globalization – indeed businesses come and go, are reconfigured and swallowed up in the process of mergers and acquisitions – but those who learn to 'travel light' and shift their investments rapidly and cleverly are the gainers in this system.

Bourdieu responds to this by suggesting that new forms of struggle must be developed. Given that ideas and knowledge are central to the new economy, albeit in constantly shifting forms, researchers themselves have a critical role to play. It is up to them to provide alternatives to the current system in ways that others can appropriate and access. This must transcend national boundaries, if it is to have any impact, drawing together diverse strands of protest and opposition and forming new collectivities and alliances.

We return to an earlier question about the role of engineering in this new economy. Are engineers and scientific researchers merely 'assets' to be employed, made redundant, redeployed if they are lucky, or rather left on the scrap heap, as financial capital decides to move on ever eastwards and upwards? The arguments presented so far suggest that this is likely to be the case. Even debates about the value of human capital and the skills and knowledge possessed by such groups, appear to carry little weight within this sort of economic configuration. In fact such solid and reliable characteristics could be seen as a liability rather than an asset, if Bauman and Bourdieu are correct. But then one must question whether it is possible for true innovation and creativity to flourish in this sort of a working environment where the institutionalization of precariousness and inbuilt instability are determining factors. Can people at work give of their best when so much is uncertain and constantly shifting? Will others be enabled to benefit from their skills and expertise? If globalization means exclusively this particular form of economic culture then it appears to be an enclosure of a potentially damaging nature.

The Issue of Work–Life Balance

Following through this example of the impact of globalization upon the engineering profession, enables us to see how the nature of work itself is being changed by the forces of the new economy. Concerns about job satisfaction and creativity, the increased pressures exerted by companies upon their employees at all levels, given the supposed weight of global competition and then the hours that are worked as a result, combine to raise questions about the well-being of those caught in this enclosure. Practical theology needs to be fully aware of this simply because it has a direct effect upon the whole of people's lives, and particularly how much spare time and energy they might have left to engage with any domestic, let alone voluntary, activity. There are further questions of social justice and the structural issues about labour relationships. But it does need to be emphasized, as writers such as Castells and Bourdieu point out, that things did not necessarily have to be this way, but are the result of certain deliberate and intentional decisions about how to respond to the changing situation.

In order to clarify this argument it is important to review the impact of such decisions upon what is now called work–life balance, and to do this by looking at figures from the UK compared with what is happening in other countries. Again it becomes clear that the impact of global forces depend upon the culture and policies of a particular nation, and the decisions which are made at a national level that can either exacerbate or ameliorate the detrimental effects of globalization.

Research carried out by Madeleine Bunting, a former religious-affairs correspondent for *The Guardian* newspaper in the UK, provides a snapshot of how work–life balance has developed in recent years (Bunting 2004). Her involvement in this issue arose because of the number of e-mails she was receiving from people who were finding it difficult to hold together the demands of work and other aspects of their lives, and so she had a pastoral rather than political motivation. The figures that she has gathered tend to support the anecdotal evidence of parish clergy that people are now working longer hours than might have been anticipated, given the high expectations that the introduction of IT and other supposed labour-saving devices were going to create a leisure society.

> Nearly 46% of men and 32% of women work more hours than they are contracted for. The problem is worst at the upper levels of the labour market, where in 2002 nearly 40% of all managers and senior officials were working more than 50 hours a week; over 30% of professionals were doing likewise. But long hours also badly affect blue-collar workers

> in fields such as construction, manufacturing and transport: between a quarter and a third of plumbers, electricians, lorry drivers and security guards are working over forty-eight hours a week. (Bunting 2004: 7)

The private sector figures are worse than those in the public sector as one might expect (17 per cent compared with 12 per cent work over 48 hours a week). Bunting concludes that the problem is a structural one, with about 4 million British workers being affected. The UK has created a culture of working long hours, comparing unfavourably with the rest of the European Union. British full-time workers put in an average of 43.6 hours per week compared with the EU average of 40.3 hours. The number of those working over 48 hours has more than doubled in the UK since 1998, from 10 per cent to 26 per cent. Between 2000 and 2002 the number of those working more than 60 hours went up by a third to 1 in 6 of all workers, and a fifth of 30 to 39 year olds – in other words those who might well be at a critical stage in their family lives – are working over 60 hours a week. One notes how this contrasts with Browning's suggestion for a reasonable working week in the previous chapter.

The gender balance is also of concern. Since 1992 the number of women working more than 48 hours has increased by 52 per cent, and the proportion working over 60 hours has more than doubled, from 6 per cent to 13 per cent. This has also an impact upon how and when people take their allotted time off, both in terms of holidays and time off during the working day itself. According to two surveys, only 44 per cent of workers take all the holiday to which they are entitled, with a reason frequently being given that people are concerned that they might jeopardize their employment prospects otherwise (Bunting 2004:10).

One might question whether any of this is significant: what are the human and social implications of these statistics? Are people in the UK happy to work longer hours, or are they simply less efficient than workers elsewhere, and so need to work longer in order to achieve comparable levels of productivity? Once again, surveys investigating job satisfaction in the UK reflect a growing trend towards frustration and an unwillingness to work such long hours. During the 1990s the number of men reporting they are 'very happy' with their working hours dropped from 35 per cent to 20 per cent and the number of women from 51 per cent to 29 per cent.

One of the key factors behind all this is a drive towards greater flexibility in working hours. Being prepared to work overnight or to be constantly available to one's employer by means of mobile phone, BlackBerry and e-mail are all starting to impinge upon the individual's non-working time. Twenty-four-hour shopping, 24-hour banking and other services have now become expectations from consumers and thus requirements for employees. This inevitably has a detrimental effect upon home life and relationships. As Bunting says:

> The knock-on effect of the 24/7 society is to deliver the final blow to those regular rituals which framed most people's lives, such as a family tea or a Sunday lunch. These regular rituals originated in the early Industrial Revolution, as a way of giving the family a role in the daily routine after it lost its pre-eminence in the organisation of economic life, with the shift from family workshop to factory. No longer the source of livelihood, the family took on tasks of structuring time, of ritual and emotional support. That is what is now being

> eroded by the timelessness of a flexible labour market which brings our working lives into direct conflict with our private family lives. (Bunting 2004: 17)

One might extrapolate from this into the impact upon community and indeed church life. The much commented upon lack of commitment and lack of regular church attendance may all be part of this erosion of routine brought about by more erratic and demanding working hours. 'Fitting everything in' is the constant complaint of many families as they struggle to balance not only their own working and domestic commitments, but also the social, educational and entertainment requirements of their offspring. Church involvement of any description becomes yet one more thing to be fitted in to an increasingly complex and fraught family timetable as the regular routines and structures of the past are undermined by frenetic and constant activity. The question of how faith groups are to respond to this changing culture is all too familiar, as has been seen in earlier chapters. Do churches collude with this new culture by offering occasional 'menu items' for busy families: do they try to work against the grain by demanding a deeper commitment, thus increasing the time pressures on busy people; or do they simply ignore these changes and continue to offer the same old package of weekly worship and hope that this will be adequate to attract enough people to guarantee a sustainable church life?

It would be possible to go on adding to these statistics, but the point is clear by now that the current emphasis upon work–life balance reflects the fact that the balance has shifted so far in favour of work, certainly in countries such as the UK, that there are damaging effects upon other aspects of people's lives. Despite the apparent levels of affluence that result from a successful engagement with the new economy, it could be argued that people feel increasingly trapped by a system that demands more working time and energy than many would prefer to give. Jobs could easily be lost abroad unless people are prepared to put the hours in – so the arguments go. Mortgages have to be paid, and that means that both parents probably have to work, even if one of them is only part-time. Maintaining both status and lifestyle – meaning one's property, cars and foreign holidays – are vital for people's sense of worth and value in this highly competitive environment, according at least to the advertisers' subliminal messages. This is the general culture that has been created as a result of a particular response to globalization and it is difficult to see any alternative to this. So the freedoms that are available are simply the limited choices determined by a standardized global culture, and which dictate where value lies and discourages alternative visions of a different life. If this is correct, then it highlights once again the challenge for faith to show how and where it offers both a critique of this, let alone a genuine practical alternative. Are there indeed thresholds to another way of being, and is there any hope that increased reflexivity might offer glimpses of other possibilities?

Chapter 8

Practical Theology and Global Ethics

Introduction

The argument of the previous seven chapters has been that the range of issues associated with globalization has a direct impact upon the subject matter of practical theology. Before bringing this to a conclusion by examining whether or not attempting to construct a global ethics and, specifically, an ethics determined or influenced by Christianity, is an appropriate response to this, it is necessary to review the general contours of the discussion. Once this has been done it will become clear how this topic is to be approached. In particular, it needs to be understood how the interlocking themes of blurred boundaries, enclosures and thresholds, and then versions of reflexivity, including a spiritual reflexivity, contribute to this task.

In Chapter 1 the idea of zombie categories was examined in order to investigate the possibility that many of the familiar themes covered by practical theology, although still of relevance, had undergone a subtle and often unacknowledged change of status. The reconfiguration now required means that the manner in which these categories appear demands a fresh interpretation and analysis using the insights of other disciplines. Practical theology has consistently drawn on its relationship with psychology, sociology, politics and philosophy as it attempts to construct adequate responses to its current context. It was also argued that the version of practical theology pursued by others and in this book is one which is transformational, or, as I have described it, as critical, emancipatory, Christian practice. The question is: how this is to be achieved in the face of globalization? Can a basis for a Christian critique of globalization be constructed from within the resources of a reconstructed practical theology?

Outline of the Argument

Many of the challenges faced by the human species as we enter this new century are global in scope. Many also fall under the heading of sustainability. Whether one is talking about access to the resources which sustain our civilization and economies, such as oil, water, food and other sources of energy, or the supposed impact of humans upon the environment, given fears about climate change and global warming, it seems that it cannot be assumed that ‘business as usual’ is going to be possible. The political pressure created by potential conflict, both international and local, over the control of and access to these resources, is a further destabilizing factor. The rapid growth of the economies of China and India, containing a third of the world’s population between them, is going to be a significant feature of the years to come. As commentators such as Smith have said, how will the existing superpower, the United States, and the fragile and developing power which is the European Union, respond to this challenge? Who will be the winners and losers in this emerging conflict, and will the current battle fields of the Middle East and Africa slowly spread across the globe as the struggles to control oil fields become of even greater importance? Although particular countries may believe that they are going to be sheltered from these conflicts, this view is clearly naïve. Economically and politically there will be repercussions for all nations. If indeed 'business as usual' is not going to be an option, where will those of faith find themselves located in this developing scenario, and are they aware of the risks attached to imagining that they will be unaffected by these changes?

A sense of place and its importance for the construction of identity is a familiar and central concern of practical theology. The importance of belonging, often associated with residence in a specific locality, has been a building block for Christian practice and self-understanding. Chapter 2 illustrates how this is being challenged and undermined by the much more fluid, porous and mobile patterns of human relatedness resulting from the global influences on social and personal life. Much church life assumes a stability and continuity of presence based on geographical places, but this is now under serious threat. It would, however, be a mistake to equate global with bad and local with good or to present these changes as essentially fragmentary. I have used Rosenau's idea of fragmegration to argue that these changes are complex, both integrating and fragmenting, and lead to a variety of responses, some of them defensive, but some also based on a critical self-understanding or reflexivity. Is it possible for the local church to be both a 'sticky place' and also a 'slippery space', thus acknowledging the ambiguities and complexities of globalization, and yet retaining a legitimate pastoral role and integrity of belief?

This discussion moves naturally into a deeper analysis of the nature of pastoral care and practice, and it is this which was presented in the Chapter 3. If the idea of a stable location can no longer be assumed as the basis for pastoral activity, and the tasks of pastoral care themselves are understood to be shared by all those of faith rather than being centred on the minister as professional, is there a new approach to the question of human identity which has been sparked off by recent developments in the global economy? These problems can be characterized as reductionist in the sense that ideas of the self as commodity or product, as consumer or even as personal project and self-creation can each be interpreted as the direct result of an economic rationality which is invading the spheres of personal development and spirituality. Faith groups may find themselves colluding with this approach, offering components for identity construction through spirituality and forms of worship, without realizing that they have been drawn into this world where even the self is 'for the time being only', and where loyalty to a specific religious institution or tradition has been superseded by the concern to create and re-create oneself on a regular basis. People now 'shop around' in the field of religion and spirituality and will not necessarily settle within a specific tradition for any length of time. The category of belonging or integrating into a particular faith community is no longer assumed to be fully operative. The key question is whether practical theology can not only work with these emerging patterns, but also establish a critique of them which engages the people concerned. This is significant when it comes to the political dimension of pastoral theology and legitimate Christian concerns with issues of global justice. Does the vision of an unconditional hospitality, for instance, provide a counterpoint to these global influences, or is it another form of collusion with global capitalism?

The impact of these questions upon worship and spirituality is of importance for practical theology, and Chapter 4 examined a possible basis for critique as proposed from within Radical Orthodoxy. Does the Eucharist provide an alternative mapping of time and space that challenges their globalized forms? Whilst agreeing with the analysis, one might question the effectiveness of a return to such a traditional understanding of worship. If worship and spirituality are increasingly disembedded as people 'shop around', such a straightforward response seems unlikely to be convincing. The work in this area carried out by the Kendal project, and also by Christopher Partridge, suggests that the process of the 'turn to subjectivity' and the creation of an 'occulture' building upon a wide variety of traditions and resources, has now taken spiritual reflexivity beyond this point. 'Alternative spiritualities' and the challenge to the authority of traditions that underlies them, are now close to becoming the norm, even for some Christians. This deregulation of religion is unlikely to be reversed as it is based on deeper cultural and intellectual roots. The blurring of boundaries between different religious traditions and resources cannot be drawn back into some sort of orthodoxy. Another feature is that fewer people are even familiar with the discourses and liturgies of traditional Christianity, so even when they search for a faith position they are likely to feel excluded by contact with traditional forms.

Chapter 5 raised the question of whether the church needs to engage with this developing culture and to develop forms of worship, spirituality and communal activity consistent with it? How is it to retain its identity and integrity if it does so, and does it run the risk of creating new constituencies which are unrelated to existing congregations? This is a challenge to such movements as the so-called 'fresh expressions' now being advocated by some within the churches, and raises the fear that they are colluding with a consumerist approach to faith. If one cannot avoid the 'spirituality supermarket', does one not need to present one's religious product on its shelves? Is there a basis for critique, one that both engages this movement and also presents an alternative approach? The idea of a spiritual reflexivity, which we have suggested can be developed from the work of Ken Wilber, allows one to analyse the development of spiritualities, and then to present the distortions and limitations of current practice. There need to be ways of moving beyond the limits of global capitalism as they impinge upon religious belief and practice. Yet this must apply also to the pluralist relativism that characterizes the supposed radical critiques launched by the new 'chattering classes', some of which are faith-based and some hostile to all forms of religion.

Chapters 6 and 7 examined two areas that traditionally fall within the remit of practical theology, that of work with children and families and the world of work. Evidence is presented from a range of disciplines to show how the global economy creates pressures upon family life and is potentially damaging to certain aspects of child development. Churches are often directly engaged with family work and increasingly drawn into working with the very young. The importance of this is underlined, but the question remains of the extent to which faith groups are colluding with a damaging social and economic order and simply attempting to ameliorate its worst impacts, or establishing an alternative approach and understanding using the insights of other disciplines. 'Selfish Capitalism' and the influence of 'impatient capital' appear to have detrimental effects upon human relationships both at home and at work. Browning proposes the concept of critical familism as the base for a Christian critique, and the need to work towards a combined 60-hour working week for married couples with children, and the importance, once again, of a notion of reflexivity within relationships. Within working life, what is the impact of the new economy upon working practices, and does this entail a lowering of job satisfaction and creativity as firms impose harsher working conditions on the grounds of needing to compete within the global economy? As everything is 'for the time being only', short-term and essentially fluid, what is the impact of this upon the social capital and norms of trust and reciprocity that have been built up in the better commercial enterprises?

What appears to emerge from this is that the major effect of globalization, particularly in the form in which it is being pursued by the new economy and the political ambitions of the Washington Consensus, is the construction of enclosures built upon reductionist understandings of what it is to be human. The self becomes both product and consumer, and the values associated with this increasingly impinge upon areas of life that might previously have been safe havens for an alternative view. These might have been the family or the gathered life of religious groups or other spheres of civil society where an ethos of care for the other through voluntary rather than commercial activity was the norm. With the blurring of boundaries that is taking place it becomes impossible to protect these areas from the influence of global capitalist values, and it is obvious that even those who claim to be offering an alternative are deluding themselves. Is there an alternative from within Christianity to this 'full spectrum dominance' exercised by global culture? Are there aspects of globalization that can be affirmed and encouraged as offering the hope of better things? Can practical theology reconstruct itself appropriately given that 'business as usual' is no longer an option?

The Idea of a Global Covenant

Exactly what types of alternative are now being proposed from within other disciplines? It is not possible to review all of these, but it is important to offer some representative ideas from a range of perspectives in order to see where a transformational practical theology might be located. One of the major suggestions comes from the field of political sociology and writers such as David Held in the UK, who has already established himself as an important commentator on globalization. Held stands in the tradition of social democracy, and his interpretations of globalization and his proposals for the future reflect that particular stance. Like others from this political persuasion he sets great store by the notion of global governance. He is optimistic that creating new structures of control and constraint at a transnational level may keep the worst effects of globalization in check.

His argument is as follows. Globalization is a complex and multi-layered phenomenon that cuts across many of the traditional boundaries of the world as it was before 1945. Since then the international order has come to depend on such notions as human rights and the supposed spread of democratic values, based upon a belief in the equal dignity and worth of all human beings. These beliefs are enshrined within complex governance systems covering areas such as financial regulation, environmental protection and calls for global justice and the eradication of poverty. Although these values are currently not being pursued by the US administration and the Washington Consensus, they may yet form the foundation for a different global order. So blurred boundaries can lead to thresholds to a better world and do not automatically create the enclosures of which we have seen such evidence in the previous chapters.

Apart from his own approach, based upon a renewed social democracy, Held points out that two other main responses have emerged. The first is that of neo-liberalism, and the second is the anti-globalization movement as seen at various demonstrations in recent years, for instance at Seattle. The neo-liberal stance is the one that currently dominates the Western world and is at the heart of the 'selfish capitalism' and 'impatient capital' that is damaging to a whole range of human relationships. It is Held's view that neither of these alternatives offers hope for a better future.

> Whereas neo-liberalism simply perpetuates existing economic and political systems and offers no substantial policies to deal with the problems of market failure, the radical anti-globalist position appears deeply naïve about the potential for locally based action to resolve, or engage with, the governance agenda generated by the forces of globalization. How can such a politics cope with the challenges posed by overlapping communities of fate? (Held 2004: 162)

A similar doubt can be voiced about the prospect of the neo-liberal position being able to tackle these challenges. If this means the USA acting unilaterally, then its consequent relationships with other nations will mean that it will be unable to deliver core global public goods such as free trade, financial stability and environmental sustainability. A unilateral US approach to foreign policy has already exacerbated international security, according to some interpretations. The alternative is a form of global social democracy. What exactly does Held mean by this?

> It is a basis for promoting the rule of international law; greater transparency, accountability and democracy in global governance; a deeper commitment to social justice; the protection and reinvention of community at diverse levels; and the transformation of the global economy into a free and fair rule-based economic order. The politics of global social democracy contain clear possibilities of dialogue between different segments of the 'pro-globalization/anti-globalization' political spectrum, although it will, of course, be contested by opinion at the extreme ends of the spectrum. (Held 2004: 163)

So somewhere in the midst of the turmoil and confusion which is globalization, the voices and action of 'sweet reason' will be able to counter the other powerful forces now at work. Held then spells out a complex and detailed series of proposals for how this would work (2004: 164–5). It is important to identify the eight principles or cosmopolitan values which he sets out. Those are: equal worth and dignity; active agency; personal responsibility and accountability; consent; collective decision-making about public matters through voting procedures; inclusiveness and subsidiarity; avoidance of serious harm; sustainability (Held 2004: 171). These detailed proposals, and the principles behind them, would form the core of a global covenant which, in an ideal world, would be binding upon the whole international community.

In many ways Held's suggestions are a re-working of the UN Millenium Development Goals which also form the base for a renewed vision of global peace and democracy, but offer a series of aspirations rather than more detailed suggestions for how these might be achieved. Once again we are talking about a long 'wish list' but here are some of the main planks of this proposal. The ambition by 2015 is to have eradicated extreme poverty and hunger; to achieve universal primary education; promote gender equality and empower women; reduce child mortality; improve maternal health; combat HIV/AIDS, malaria and other diseases; ensure environmental sustainability; develop a global partnership for development (quoted in Held 2004: 64).

What is one to make of such proposals? On one level it is impossible to argue against them, because nobody would probably openly admit to being opposed to them, even if it is was in their interests to be so. The list is indeed representative of what have become the new Western democratic conventional wisdom and the accepted goals of future development. The problem is knowing what to do with such 'wish lists' once they are established within the global public forum. Is there any way, in practical terms, that they are likely to be accepted by governments as the criteria by which both domestic and international policies and actions are to be judged? Even if a majority of governments were to accept them, how would the global community deal with those that refused to do so? Although they are indeed fine aspirations, what is the reality of global political life, and how would governments impose such a wide-ranging set of ambitions upon major global players such as transnational companies? The questions proliferate, but the problem is how to turn universal proposals, which reflect the ideals of a very specific group of people, working from within a particular context, into a universally accepted set of policies that might have some practical implications. This is a charter or covenant that might be accepted by reasonable people, but then, even with reasonable people, such principles might lose out when other personal or collective interests are at stake. Are not Held and his colleagues from within global social democratic circles simply too optimistic? Where is the evidence on how structures of global governance work in practice and how effective is this likely to be?

The argument of this book is that the criteria proposed in Chapter 5, on globalization and spirituality, need to be brought into play at this point in order that practical theology might evaluate ideas such as Held's of a global covenant. Those criteria would not argue against such a covenant by attempting to return to a form of faith that is opposed to the exercise of reason with the public realm, but would point to the limitations and dangers of an approach which failed to take into account the other levels at which human being operate, both the pre-autonomous level, where the less reasonable aspects of behaviour and motivation come into play, and the post-autonomous level or that of a reflexive spirituality, where a vision of what human beings might become which goes beyond reason illuminates the future. Hence ideas such as Held's do indeed have a role to play within public debate, but it would be naïve to claim that they are more than a step along the way.

A Global Ethic or Global Ethics?

Another related approach which might appear to build upon ideas such as Held's, is that it is possible to establish a code of ethics which would be global in scope. However, before going too far down this route, it is as well to recognize that there is an ambiguity in this suggestion. The notion that there could be a global ethic in the sense of a code that would be universally accepted, carries with it the same problems as Held's concept of a global covenant. Under what conditions could this become a reality, and what would have to change in order for it to become so? Another possible meaning is that globalization itself becomes the subject matter of an ethical inquiry. This might or might not yield an ethical response that commands wider support or understanding, and would be certain to be based upon a specific set of ethical assumptions or a particular moral code. The outcome of this would be an 'ethics of globalization' much as this book has set out to establish a practical theology of globalization. A further possibility, and one that has yet to receive much attention, is that globalization itself alters the nature and subject matter of ethics, in which case there could be a 'globalization of ethics' rather than the other way around. Again there are parallels with this book in that I am arguing that globalization has indeed changed certain key aspects of practical theology and that, whether this is recognized or not, practical theology has now been globalized.

It is clear that this is a complex discussion and that clarity is essential in pursuing this subject. One commentator has helpfully categorized existing approaches in order to identify where they stand within this spectrum of possibilities (Dower 2007: 83). So, for instance, Kung's attempt to argue that there is a core of values that cuts across all the major world religions, appears to suggest that global problems demand a response from a global ethic in the sense of a shared set of beliefs and practices. These may not yet exist, but could be developed, building upon what is agreed to be common across faith boundaries. The danger is that faith is reduced to a lowest common denominator and individual aspects of specific faith are abandoned and sacrificed in the search for a global religious ethics. Who would accept the end result and how would they convince others to do likewise? An alternative is that a specific faith-based ethical approach might be applied to the range of issues associated with globalization without any expectation that others would necessarily share the values underlying it. Or perhaps one of the social sciences might attempt to establish that there is a different type of core area that does indeed command universal interest or agreement, on the basis of which further discussions can then proceed. Amaryta Sen's interpretation of human capabilities, and the definitions of human well-being that stem from this, are now being used by United Nations organizations in order to evaluate development economics, for instance, and these also appear in theological discussions of globalization (Atherton 2003; Alkire 2005).

For the sake of completeness there are a number of potential meanings that could be described as the globalization of ethics. Global issues and problems might become seen as a recognized area of enquiry for ethics, so global ethics stands alongside other subjects such as medical ethics or environmental ethics and is possibly related to them. The range of issues involved could be world poverty, foreign intervention, immigration, international trade rules, debt relief for poorer nations and so on. So one's ethical horizons are expanded through greater exposure to what is happening in other parts of the world. One can see that this process is now well underway within some faith-based circles. This might also involve an acceptance that an ethics which was global in principle has now also become global in practice, as the global scope of such problems as climate change becomes clear. Yet it is possible that familiar concepts within ethics are themselves altered and expanded by their encounter with global issues. Thus ideas such as responsibility for others, the nature of community and relationships, notions of care and neighbourhood, now require a different understanding in this expanded context. As and when this happens there are parallels with the argument that practical theology needs to review its established categories and to accept that some of these have become zombie categories. One cannot simply apply the existing ideas to this new context as the nature of the changes requires something more radical. There is still the inevitable question of the extent to which any of this becomes shared by a wider range of people, especially those who espouse other values and beliefs. How global is global?

It is at this point that the debate gets even more complex as one asks whether a global ethic in the sense of a universally shared perspective is either possible or desirable. Of course, it depends on the content of such an ethic. A global ethic might be presented which defends precisely the neo-liberal stance that is damaging to human relationships. If that were to be contested, it would require a deeper commitment by all to engage in open and democratic discussion of the full range of possible ethical frameworks emerging from different traditions and cultures. How would that be agreed, let alone enforced globally, unless something like Held's global covenant became a reality? Yet if it is not going to be possible to establish either some means of conducting those debates globally, let alone a set of values that all might begin to share or move towards, the consequences of the ensuing conflicts given the global scale of the problems we face, themselves become disturbing and unthinkable. In which case a global ethic – provided it is the right one of course – sounds an attractive proposition.

The only clear conclusion that emerges from this is that one cannot even begin the discussion about global ethics or a global ethic until one has established a normative base, agreed more widely or otherwise. Any discussion of this kind has to begin somewhere, and has to establish a set of criteria on which to ground ethical judgements. On that level, practical theology must engage with the question of its own values and beliefs, if it is to contribute to this debate about global ethics.

Privileged Sites of Resistance

Another possible approach is to be found within more radical left wing political theory and depends to a large degree on establishing or presupposing that there is a privileged site of resistance from where genuine alternatives to the current form of Western global capitalism may be launched. The Marxist tendencies in this are clear, but these ideas come from thinkers who see themselves as post-Marxists and are related to other more recent strands of philosophical thought. It is important that practical theology engages with this discussion, as it needs to recognize that the notion that one can simply reform global capitalism, or create structures which somehow keep it in check, can itself be criticized on the grounds that it colludes with the current system rather than substantially changing it. Is this enough for a practical theology that claims to be truly transformational? If it is not, then what more radical attempts might be made to undermine the status quo, and is there any basis on which Christians might learn from or engage with such ideas?

Marxism, in its traditional mode, presented the proletariat as a privileged site of resistance. This stratum of society would be where the revolution emerged, as they were the ones most directly disadvantaged by the growing dominance of capitalism. Whilst that concept no longer holds the imagination of left-wing thinkers and activists in the way that it once did, the general idea that there will be an equivalent to emerge from this phase of capitalist expansion still constitutes a key part of post-Marxist theory. The enclosure–threshold dynamic that I have drawn on at various points in the book in part at least derives from the work of Hardt and Negri, and their more recent work argues that there is indeed a way of identifying where resistance to global capitalism will develop. The concept of full spectrum dominance mentioned earlier is taken from their latest book, and is their attempt to show how the influence of the USA, in particular, is more than just military or political but works its way through all levels of culture and society. Military might has to be combined with social, economic, political, psychological and ideological control (Hardt and Negri 2005: 53).

It is their contention that this exercise of power creates its own counter-resistance and will lead to thresholds that will challenge the enclosures created by such a strategy:

> Dominance, no matter how multi-dimensional, can never be complete and is always contradicted by resistance. Military strategy here runs up against a philosophical problem. A sovereign power is always two-sided: a dominating power always relies on the consent or submission of the dominated. The power of sovereignty is thus always limited, and this limit can always potentially be transformed into resistance, a point of vulnerability, a threat. (Hardt and Negri 2005: 54)

The question that follows from this is how and where such sites of resistance become a reality: how is the potential actually realized? Their answer to this is the idea of the 'multitude' (the title of their 2005 book). They present the multitude as an active social subject, acting from a whole series of different situations and contexts, and yet still capable of being the spearhead of new forms of democracy. They do not equate this with the working class in a classical Marxist sense, although they do appear to mean all those who are at the sharp end of current global capitalist production. This category now has to be extended to include workers who are caught at higher levels of economic activity, for example, those involved in communications technology and in the various forms of bio-political production that now dominates Western economies in particular. Control of people's lives through control of their bodies and their lifestyles is a characteristic of global capitalism, and another symptom of the full spectrum dominance exercised by commercial forces.

More orthodox Marxist theorists challenge this view, and prefer to highlight the role of traditional wage labour as the spearhead of any potential revolution, as this is the real cutting edge of capitalist exploitation (Callinicos 2006: 146). However, the details of this internal debate are of less interest to practical theology than an overall assessment of whether Hardt and Negri's argument convinces us that there is a genuine alternative. The problem with the idea of the multitude is that it is made up of a series of singularities or individual points of resistance that would have to rely on networks and essentially fluid and unstable means of coordination in order to establish a substantial counter-movement. Other than suggesting that some form of spontaneous coordination of these singularities will emerge, Hardt and Negri present no further practical strategy or structures to show how the resistance to sovereign power would take shape.

What they are saying is that the seeds of the revolution are always already present within the current structures, and that they will come to the surface in an almost mystical manner, as and when the time is right. Callinicos argues that there is a quasi-theological dimension to this, a sort of secularized concept of grace where the alternative breaks through the existing reality at points which cannot be predicted or controlled, and that the only response is to hope that they will merge into a more general movement. There are however both philosophical and political problems with this.

> In this non-hierarchical 'smooth world', where the 'equality of being' is increasingly realized, there is no longer any unevenness, any 'weak links', any specific points where contradictions accumulate and capital is particularly vulnerable. Consequently, strategy no longer has any leverage. The reason why this doesn't matter too much is that liberation is always already here. (Callinicos 2006: 149)

In other words, there is not enough substance to Hardt and Negri's theories to illustrate how a genuine alternative could emerge, or to even show why this might happen, given their apparent view that what already exists constitutes the revolution even if only in embryonic form. This is very interesting from a theological perspective, as it has implications for how much real change or transformation a practical theology might be suggesting if it holds to the view that God's grace is always already at work in human life and needs no further substantial change in order to be effective. If this is the case then what is there left to work towards and how can theology present a more structured critique of global capitalism. It might 'nibble away at the edges' or propose certain marginal reforms and improvements but without ever challenging the essential power structures that dominate people's lives. The status quo remains firmly in place with a few minor adjustments and victories achieved here and there.

It would appear that Hardt and Negri's proposal for a privileged site of resistance in the multitude carries no real hope of achieving significant change and that they fail to answer their own question of how the enclosures of current global capitalism can be seriously punctured by the discovery of thresholds to a better system.

There is a further problem that comes to the surface through Hardt and Negri's work which is that of whether or not the revolutionary vanguard are setting out to take power, or rather to undermine the very structures of power. If it is the first there is always the danger that one dominant or authoritarian group will be replaced by another and that nothing substantial will be changed. If it is the second, there needs to be some positive description of the alternative that will take its place, if this strategy is to be convincing. Another aspect of this might be that the sites of resistance are no more than spaces carved out from within the existing system and where people claim that they operating according to different rules, being counter-cultural or the equivalent. In which case it might be argued that such spaces are convenient locations where dissidents can continue to exist without seriously challenging the status quo. Practical theology cannot escape these questions, if it is going to claim to be transformative. What is the nature and scope of the transformation for which it hopes, and what are the signs that it is either already a possibility, or that it might be realized at some future date, however distant? Either one starts from the present moment and the current situation and aims to either build upon existing signs of promise or to identify where these might emerge, or one envisions some radically different future that depends on a new order breaking in from the outside, and that might not even be recognizable from where we are now.

Žižek, a radical, post-Marxist, Slovenian, political philosopher, argues that Hardt and Negri are essentially too Marxist in their outlook, believing that the seeds of the revolution are already identifiable within the capitalist system. The internal contradictions of capitalism are what will eventually tear it apart and release the energy for a new order to emerge. The problem with this is that it might be the internal contradictions that perpetuate the capitalist order, so no real escape is possible.

> In short, what Marx overlooked is that – to put it in classical Derridean terms – this inherent obstacle/antagonism, as the 'condition of impossibility' of the full deployment of the production forces, is simultaneously its 'condition of possibility': if we abolish the obstacle, the inherent contradiction of capitalism, we do not get the fully unleashed drive to productivity finally delivered of its impediment, we lose precisely this productivity that seemed to be generated and simultaneously thwarted by capitalism – if we take away the obstacle, the very potential thwarted by this obstacle dissipates. (Žižek 2006: 266)

Where does this leave the prospects for a real challenge to global capitalism? Does it mean that any opposition is pointless and will simply lead back to the starting point, or that one ruling group will be substituted for another without any substantial change? Are there other groups or individuals who might hold the key to an alternative future? Žižek has a challenging suggestion to present.

> There is, however, a privileged site in this series: what if the new proletariat position is that of the inhabitants of the slums in the new megalopolises? The explosive growth of slums in recent decades, especially in Third World megalopolises from Mexico City and other

> Latin American capitals through Africa (Lagos, Chad) to India, China, the Philippines, and Indonesia, is perhaps the crucial geopolitical event of our times ... Since, sometime very soon, the urban population of the earth will outnumber the rural population, and since slum dwellers will make up the majority of the urban population, we are by no means dealing with a marginal phenomenon. We are thus witnessing the rapid growth of a population outside state control, living in conditions outside the law, in dire need of minimal forms of self-organization. (Žižek 2006: 268)

These groups are part of the global economy as they form members of the workforce, and are also symptomatic of the way in which global capitalism operates, but what sort of ideology or public movement is capable of mobilizing them, or appeals directly to their circumstances? One answer, of course, is fundamentalist forms of religion. Pentecostal Christianity for instance, which meets people's basic needs while offering them the prospect of a different world. Is this an emerging site of resistance?

What characterizes these groups is that they are both enclosed within the global system and yet also marginalized from it, both inside and outside. Even more than the refugee (according to Žižek) the slum dweller is the 'living dead' of global capitalism, pushed into the space of the 'out of control', beyond the exercise of the normal powers of state bureaucracies and the military. They are the counter-class to the other newly emerging class of managers, IT consultants, academics and journalists which perceives itself as the vanguard of winners in the global system, but which is firmly locked inside it and dependent upon its continued success, even for their capacity to protest against it.

Another way of describing this is to say that there are marginalized groups who slip between the structures of the system with its regular blurring of boundaries – they end up fitting nowhere. In the culture of success which predominates they are the clear failures. If they have the capacity or energy to reflect upon that location, such a reflexivity would not be based upon deep intellectual self-analysis, but rather upon an awareness of exclusion and even failure. Is this section of society the 'internal other' or inherent contradiction of global capitalism that will form the seedbed of substantive challenge and change?

It is not obvious that this answer progresses the possibilities any further than Hardt and Negri's hopes placed upon the multitude. After all, how are such varied and disparate people to be drawn together, let alone to form any serious political opposition to current structures or to evolve a substantive alternative political system? They may indeed escape the enclosures, up to a point, but to what exactly do they form a threshold other than to a poverty stricken and excluded future? Žižek may be correct that they are the contemporary equivalent of the proletariat, but they seem no better placed to bring about a revolution than their supposed predecessors. It is hard to imagine the dispossessed of global capitalism paving the way to a new world order, even though they may be a site of resistance.

Reconstructing Practical Theology

How is one to draw together the different strands of investigation that have been pursued so far? What would a reconstructed practical theology look like, and how will it differ from what has gone before? The argument has been that in each of the characteristic areas that form this discipline, whether that is worship, pastoral care, work with young people or concerns for the world of work, the impact of the changes being brought about by globalization require a rethinking of the familiar categories. They are in danger of being 'the living dead' or zombie categories that appear not to have altered and yet are no longer as they were. Only by drawing upon the insights of other disciplines can practical theology improve its own self understanding and equip itself to tackle this new context.

It is left however with the central question of how it is to evaluate the changes that are taking place. In each area it has been seen that what is at stake is a view on what it is to be human. To what extent is a sense of identity determined or shaped by belonging to a specific geographical area? What are the implications of reducing human beings to either consumers or products, and how do worship and spirituality get drawn into this movement? How is the health and well-being of children and families damaged by becoming subject to the rigours of the new economy with its demands upon time and energy? How might future conflicts over access to resources influence political action, and the dangers of new battle lines both within and between nations, affect the ways in which individuals and groups view possible opponents? It is the argument of this book that practical theology must deepen its analysis and its vision of human nature (as it could become and is meant to be) if it is to effectively engage with these threats to its current understanding.

As alternative approaches to the subject of globalization have been reviewed – and there are others that could have been drawn upon had space permitted – the same question is clearly to the fore. The idea of a global covenant and the social democratic or cosmopolitan stance that lies behind it is important to the developing debate, but I have suggested that practical theology should keep a critical distance from these concepts, arguing that they depend upon an inadequate notion of human nature, failing to take into account both the pre-autonomous and post-autonomous levels of human development. Reason itself is necessary, but not sufficient, to tackle the problems we face. Similarly, it seems premature for practical theology to become embroiled in the complexities of attempting to establish a global ethic, even though it is certainly involved in developing an ethical interpretation of globalization from a specific stance. Practical theology may learn from the various suggestions for a more radical political response emerging from Post-Marxists such as Hardt and Negri, and Žižek, but should be wary of signing up to any political programme as such, particularly as no obvious or workable large-scale alternative to global capitalism has yet to emerge and, even if it did, it would be inappropriate for theology to identify with these movements.

A continued engagement, retaining a critical distance, is required, in order to understand the limitations of and damage being done by the current form of global capitalism, but learning from the analyses does not entail agreeing with the proposed solutions. Practical theology requires its own normative base for a critique of what is happening, but one that does not remain simply, or even safely, within the fold of its own tradition. As I have argued in Chapter 5, the situation has gone beyond that. Ideas which fall under the heading of a spiritual reflexivity or a reflexive spirituality – and I realize that I have used the terms interchangeably, and that reveals a certain ambiguity of meaning that reflects the developing and shifting interpretations here – seem to be the most likely candidates for a normative base. I am aware that others are already employing terms such as well-being in order to progress this debate (Atherton 2008), and I have used this myself on other occasions (Reader 2006), but I believe that the ensuing discussion about definitions could deflect energy from the central issues. The term needs attention because it is being increasingly used in secular debates and thus practical theology will have to enter this discourse, but underlying it must still be a concept of what it is to be human, or of the direction and hope for future human development. This is where my proposals for a post-autonomous level of that development become crucial.

How does this contribute to the critical assessment of globalization?

First of all it guards against the potentially regressive tendencies of faith-based responses to threats to identity which can result in closed and fundamentalist reactions to the level of global risk now faced. In other words, one of the most powerful attractions of belonging to an enclosed and exclusive religious grouping is that it offers a supposedly safe haven from the external changes of globalization and a rationale for rejecting the demands of others when it comes to accessing diminishing resources.

If the result of climate change, or even the economic growth of China and India, is increasing conflict over access to key resources such as oil and water, then battle lines will be drawn up between different nations and groups and religious differences become a means of doing this. According to the criteria offered in Chapter 5 this represents a regressive understanding of faith which ought to be able to take people beyond such rigid distinctions and differences.

Then there is the further question of ways in which environmental arguments might well be employed by politicians as a means of encouraging people to accept the sacrifices in standards of living and access to the goods of global capitalism that may result from economic and political changes. I have argued elsewhere (Reader 2005) that one of the agendas behind UK politicians' emphasis upon sustainable communities, community cohesion and the role of faith-based groups in providing social capital, is the fear that social unrest will follow the realization that the goods of global capitalism, taken for granted by many, will have to be rationed. Simply doing this through the market and price mechanisms is unlikely to be sufficient, as the sacrifices required will hit the middle classes, as well as those already closer to the bottom of the economic ladder. Encouraging people to save energy and to reduce their levels of consumption generally by using environmental and religious arguments and motivations, is an obvious strategy for governments to pursue as they attempt to limit the risks of social disorder.

Perhaps the critical and immediate challenge facing Christians in this developing scenario where 'business as usual' is no longer an option, is how and where they will locate themselves within the environmental debate. Many have already taken on board the apparent need to respond to the threats posed by climate change, and every subsequent bout of extreme weather or external activity which can be attributed to this cause will add to the pressures to adopt radical changes. The problem comes when this requires genuine sacrifices in terms of lifestyles and living standards. My suspicion is that faith groups already committed to the environmental cause will be encouraged and then possibly appropriated by a political agenda which promotes sacrifices of this nature – of course leaving the global elites to enjoy their access to the goods of global capitalism for that much longer. How might a Christian understanding of social justice cut through this debate?

Green or environmental spiritualities which are perceived to be at the cutting edge of faith development, may fit neatly into this political agenda, so how might it be possible to retain the critical distance required by a reflexive spirituality? This is where the ideas derived from Wilber, and suggested in Chapter 5, become crucial. To realize that an environmentally aware and motivated spirituality is not the end point of human spiritual development becomes vital. To understand that politicians and others pursue other agendas which can appear to cohere with a religious interpretation, but may actually present views which challenge and undermine a developing reflexive spirituality, is central to the task of a reconstructed practical theology. This can only be founded upon a normative basis for critique that encapsulates a more profound notion of human development and identity.

The pre-autonomous level of human development, where we continue to be driven by and are under the influence of internal forces of which we are not even aware, (and probably never can be) is still in operation in the decisions we make and the paths we pursue. No amount of reflexivity or self awareness will ever fully counter these internal forces, but we can at least know that this is part of what it is to be human. The idea of autonomy which proposes that humans can be fully aware of and in control of their actions, and then pursue policies and courses of action rationally worked out and deployed (as in the concept of global governance and a global covenant), is not to be dismissed, and needs to be part of a reasoned and openly debated response to the challenges we face. But this must involve a realistic analysis of how humans exercise power and use ideas that promote their own self interest, and this is where the work of philosophers such as Habermas, and Marx before him, is so crucial. Autonomy is not itself the end of the road for human development, and the difficult and somewhat obscure notion of a post-autonomous level, based upon a notion of spiritual reflexivity must come into play as providing the (messianic) vision of what humans are capable of becoming. We may only be at the beginning of this understanding, but unless it is possible to actively pursue this path, then the challenges that face humanity as a result of global forces, both human induced and otherwise, may simply overwhelm us. Practical theology with both eyes fixed on this horizon, has a part to play in averting this threatening future.

Bibliography

Alkire, Sabina

2005, *Valuing Freedoms: Sen's Capability Approach and Poverty Reduction* (Oxford: Oxford University Press).

Archbishop of Canterbury's Commission on Urban Priority Areas

1985, *Faith in the City: A Call for Action by Church and Nation* (London: Church House Publishing).

Atherton, John

2003, *Marginalization* (London: SCM Press).

2008, *Religion and Transcendence of Capitalism* (forthcoming).

Atherton, John and Hannah Skinner (eds)

2007, *Through the Eye of a Needle: Theological Conversations Over Political Economy* (London: Epworth).

Barley, Linda

2006, *Churchgoing Today* (London: Church House Publishing).

Bauman, Zygmunt

1993, *Postmodern Ethics* (Oxford: Blackwell).

2000, *Liquid Modernity* (Oxford: Blackwell).

2006, *Liquid Life* (Cambridge: Polity Press).

Beck, Ulrich

1992, *Risk Society: Towards a New Modernity* (London: Sage Publications).

2000, *World Risk Society* (Cambridge: Polity Press).

2006, *Cosmopolitan Vision* (Cambridge: Polity Press).

Beck, Ulrich, Anthony Giddens and Scott Lash

1994, *Reflexive Modernization: Politics, Tradition and Aesthetics in the Modern Social Order* (Cambridge: Polity Press).

Beck, Ulrich and Elisabeth Beck-Gernsheim

2002, *Individualization* (London: Sage Publications).

Berger, Peter

1967, *A Rumour of Angels* (London: Penguin).

Bourdieu, Pierre

2003, *Firing Back: Against the Tyranny of the Market 2* (London: Verso).

Browning, Don S.

2006, *Christian Ethics and the Moral Psychologies* (Grand Rapids, MI: Wm. B. Eerdmans).

2007, *Equality and the Family: A Fundamental, Practical Theology of Children, Mothers, and Fathers in Modern Societies* (Grand Rapids, MI: Wm. B. Eerdmans).

Bruce, Stephen

2003, 'The Demise of Christianity', in Grace Davie, Paul Heelas and Linda Woodhead (eds), *Predicting Religion: Christian, Secular and Alternative Futures* (Aldershot: Ashgate), pp. 53–63.

Bunting, Madeleine

2004, *Willing Slaves: How the Overwork Culture is Ruling our Lives* (London: HarperCollins).

Callinicos, Alex

2006, *The Resources of Critique* (Cambridge: Polity Press).

Castells, Manuel

2001, *The Rise of the Network Society: The Information Age, Economy, Society and Culture*, vol. 1 (Oxford: Blackwell).

Castree, Noel, Neil M Coe, Kevin Ward and Michael Samers

2004, *Spaces of Work: Global Capitalism and Geographies of Labour* (London: Sage Publications).

Cavanaugh, William T.

2002, *Theopolitical Imagination* (London: T&T Clark).

Commission on Urban Life and Faith

2006, *Faithful Cities: A Call for Celebration, Vision and Justice* (London: Methodist Publishing House and Church House Publishing).

Damasio, R. Antonio.

2000, *The Feeling of What Happens: Body,Emotion and the making of Consciousmess* (London: Heinemann).

Derrida, Jacques.

1994, *Spectres of Marx: The State of the Debt, the Work of Mourning and the New International* (London: Routledge).

Dower, Nigel

2007, 'The Challenge of Global Ethics: Is a Global Ethic either Possible or Desirable', in Carl-Henric Grenholm and Normunds Kamergrauzis (eds), *Sustainable Development and Global Ethics* (Stockholm: Uppsala Universitet Press), pp. 79–94.

Fishman, Ted C.

2005, *China Inc: The Relentless Rise of the Next Great Superpower* (London: Simon and Shuster).

Fontana, David

2003, *Psychology, Religion, and Spirituality* (Oxford: Blackwell).

Fowler, James

1981, *Stages of Faith: The Psychology of Human Development and the Quest for Meaning* (San Francisco: Harper and Row).

Fromm, Erich

1985, *The Fear of Freedom* (London: Routledge).

Giddens, Anthony

1991, *Modernity and Self Identity: Self and Society in the Late Modern Age* (Cambridge: Polity Press).

Goleman, Daniel

2004, *Destructive Emotions: And How we can Overcome Them* (London: Bloomsbury Publishing).

Graham, Elaine

1996, *Transforming Practice: Pastoral Theology in an Age of Uncertainty* (London: Mowbray).

2002, *Representations of the Post/Human: Monsters, Aliens and Others in Popular Culture* (Manchester: Manchester University Press).

Graham, Elaine, Heather Walton and Frankie Ward

2005, *Theological Reflections: Methods*, vol. 1 (London: Epworth).

Granfield, David

1991, *Heightened Consciousness: The Mystical Difference* (Mahwah, NJ: Paulist Press).

Habermas, Jürgen

1981, *Knowledge and Human Interests* (London: Heinemann Educational Books).

1984, *The Theory of Communicative Action*, vol. 1: *Reason and the Rationalization of Society* (London: Heinemann Educational Books).

1987, *The Theory of Communicative Action*, vol. 2: *The Critique of Functionalist Reason* (Cambridge: Polity Press).

Hardt, Michael and Antonio Negri

2001, *Empire* (Cambridge, MA: Harvard University Press).

2005, *Multitude* (London: Penguin).

Heelas, Paul and Linda Woodhead

2005, *The Spiritual Revolution: Why Religion is giving way to Spirituality* (Oxford: Blackwell).

Held, David

2004, *Global Covenant: The Social Democratic Alternative to the Washington Consensus* (Cambridge: Polity Press).

Held, David and Anthony McGrew (eds)

2000, *The Global Transformations Reader: An Introduction to the Globalization Debate* (Cambridge: Polity Press).

2002, *Governing Globalization, Power, Authority and Global Governance* (Cambridge: Polity Press).

Heymann, Jody

2007, *Forgotten Families: Ending the Growing Crisis Confronting Children and Working Parents in the Global Economy* (Oxford: Oxford University Press).

Hopkinson, Jill

2005, *Seeds in Holy Ground: A Workbook for Rural Churches* (n.p.: ACORA Publishing on behalf of the Mission and Public Affairs Council of the Archbishops' Council of the Church of England).

Howard, Sue and David Welbourne

2004, *The Spirit at Work Phenomenon* (London: Azure).

Hutton, Will

2007, *The Writing on the Wall: China and the West in the 21st Century* (London: Little, Brown and Co.).

Inge, John
2003, *A Christian Theology of Place* (Aldershot: Ashgate).
James, Oliver
2007, *Affluenza: How to be Successful and Stay Sane* (London: Random House).
Janzten, Grace M.
1995, *Power, Gender and Christian Mysticism* (Cambridge: Cambridge University Press).
Johnston, R.J. et al. (eds)
2000, *The Dictionary of Human Geography* (Oxford: Blackwell).
Lynch, Gordon
2005, *Understanding Theology and Popular Culture* (Oxford: Blackwell).
Milbank, John.
1990, *Theology and Social Theory: Beyond Secular Reason* (Oxford: Blackwell).
Negri, Antonio
2004, *Time for Revolution* (London: Continuum).
Northwest Development Agency
2003, *Faith in England's Northwest: The Contribution made by Faith Communities to Civil Society in the Region* (n.p.: Northwest Development Agency, 2003).
Partridge, Christopher
2004, *The Re-Enchantment of the West*, vol. 1: *Alternative Spiritualities, Sacralization, Popular Culture and Occulture* (London: T&T Clark).
Reader, John
1987, 'Rural Theology: Where do We Start?', in Richard Lewis and Andrew Talbot-Ponsonby, *The People, the Land and the Church* (Hereford: Hereford Diocesan Board of Finance), pp. 48–55.
1994, *Local Theology: Church and Community in Dialogue* (London: SPCK).
1997, *Beyond All Reason: The Limits of Post-Modern Theology* (Cardiff: Aureus Publishing).
2005, *Blurred Encounters: A Reasoned Practice of Faith* (Cardiff: Aureus Publishing).
2006, *Apocalyptic Localism or Sustainable Communities? An Emerging Role for Faith-Based (Religious) Capital* (William Temple Foundation Occasional Paper, 33: Manchester: William Temple Foundation).
Rosenau, James
2003, *Distant Proximities: Dynamics Beyond Globalization* (Princeton, NJ: Princeton University Press).
Schweiker, William
2000, 'Responsibility in the World of Mammon: Theology, Justice and Transnational Corporations', in Max. L Stackhouse and Peter J. Paris (eds), *Religion and the Powers of the Common Life: God and Globalization*, vol. 1 (Harrisburg, PA: Trinity Press International), pp. 105–139.
Sennett, Richard
2006, *The Culture of the New Capitalism* (New Haven, CT: Yale University Press).

Skinner, Hannah

2005, *A Place of Refuge: A Positive Approach to Asylum Seekers and Refugees in the UK* (London: Church House Publishing).

Smith, Dennis

2006, *Globalization: The Hidden Agenda* (Cambridge: Polity Press).

Stern, Nicholas.

2006, *The Stern Report* (London: HMSO).

Swinton, John and Harriet Mowat

2006, *Practical Theology and Qualitative Research* (London: SCM Press).

Thompson, Ross A.

2006, *Updating Moral Development Theory, Early Conscience* (Symposium Paper on Personality and Moral Character at Notre Dame University given on 12–14 October).

2007, *Testimony given to the US Congress House Committee on Education and Labour, Subcommittee on Early Childhood, Elementary and Secondary Education on February 28th, 2007*; available at www.house.gov/ed_workforce/testimony/022807/RossThompsontestimony (accessed 10 March 2008).

Underhill, Evelyn

1993, *Mysticism: The Nature and Development of Spiritual Consciousness* (Oxford: Oneworld Publications).

UNICEF Report

2007, *Harnessing Globalization for Children*; available at www.unicef-irc.org/research/ESP/globalization (accessed 10 March 2008)

Wilber, Ken

1983, *A Sociable God: Towards a New Understanding of Religion* (Boulder, CO: Shambhala Publications).

2000, *Integral Psychology: Consciousness, Spirit, Psychology, Therapy* (Boston MA: Shambhala Publications).

Wilkinson, Richard G.

2005, *The Impact of Inequality: How to make Sick Societies Healthier* (London: Routledge).

Woodward, James and Stephen Pattison

2000, *The Blackwell Reader in Pastoral and Practical Theology* (Oxford: Blackwell).

Žižek, Slavoj

2006, *The Parallax View* (Cambridge, MA: MIT Press).

Index